Sarah

Endorsements

Are We There Yet? The Journey into The Presence Of God is one of the most comprehensive and easy–to–understand books written about God's plan to restore man to himself through his son, Jesus Christ.

Using the types and shadows of Tabernacle of Moses, Sarah Ramsey has done a marvelous job of simplifying the foundation of Christian faith, and that is, what did Jesus come to do? This foundation must be laid in order to build a successful Christian life.

If you work carefully through the book, you will be thoroughly grounded in the greatest revelation given to mankind: Who we are in Christ and who Christ is in us.

In a time when mankind has apparently lost his mooring to anything steadfast and absolute, *Are We There Yet* comes along to re–establish the key foundation under the Body of Christ. Every Christian worker serious about their service for the gospel should add this foundational work to their library.

—Joe McGee
President Joe McGee Ministries/
Faith For Families

As president of Derek Prince Ministries USA I want to express my gratitude to my friend Sarah Ramsey for so adeptly applying in this book the principles Derek Prince so often taught. Our hope and trust is that Sarah's in–depth examination of the pathway into the presence of God will inspire many to begin and complete this valuable journey—and then to abide in His presence once they have arrived there.

—Dick Leggatt
President Derek Prince Ministries

I have known Sarah Ramsey and her family for twenty years. She and her husband, Paul, have been true friends and mentors in the faith. Sarah has a contagious love for Christ and His presence. She has personally mentored and discipled dozens of ladies and families in the instruction of righteousness. She is known in our community as a virtuous woman and one who walks intimately with the Lord. Sarah has a keen insight into the workings of the Holy Spirit, and her personal prayer life is honored and emulated by countless others. It is an honor for me to recommend Sarah Ramsey and her gift to you.

—Eddie Turner
Pastor

ARE

Journey Into

WE

the Presence

THERE

of God

YET?

Sarah Lynne Ramsey

ARE

Journey Into

WE

the Presence

THERE

of God

YET?

Tate Publishing *& Enterprises*

Published by Tate Publishing & Enterprises, LLC
127 E. Trade Center Terrace | Mustang, Oklahoma 73064 USA
1.888.361.9473 | www.tatepublishing.com

Tate Publishing is committed to excellence in the publishing industry. The company reflects the philosophy established by the founders, based on Psalm 68:11,
"The Lord gave the word and great was the company of those who published it."

Book design copyright © 2009 by Tate Publishing, LLC. All rights reserved.
Cover design by Amber Gulilat
Interior design by Lindsay B. Behrens

Published in the United States of America

ISBN: 978-1-60799-462-6
1. Religion / Biblical Studies / Exegesis & Hermeneutics
2. Religion / Christian Life / Spiritual Growth
09.06.09

Dedication

To You, all–wise God—

The One who loves me and makes all provision for
me to get where You are in Jesus, my Lord.

The One who is in love with me and the One I love.

The One my soul has longed for and
the One who satisfies my soul!

Acknowledgments

To my loving and supportive husband and my children and my children's children, who have lived through the "birthing" of *Are We There Yet? Journey into the Presence of God*. My sweet family is the provision of precious Abba Father.

Elizabeth Ramsey was the first one who told me to write down what I was being taught.

Carol Buckner caught the vision at a conference I was teaching and got this journey started; because Carol obeyed, she was the initiator of this project.

Eileen Cunliffe picked up the ball and endured to carry the ball into the end zone. She is a keeper! I can't express how much Carol and Eileen have contributed to this book.

Susannah you always and forever encourage me and Jenny Lynne, you came to help me get all the ducks in line and finish.

And to all of you who have made the journey into the Holy of Holies with me, encouraged and stood with me, and believed.

When I was learning how to follow the pattern of entering in to God's presence, the Lord gave me three teachers who knew the way: Derek Prince, Andrew

Murray, and Judson Cornwall. I am forever grateful for their teaching; they have helped me know Jesus better.

Table of Contents

Foreword

As an author, my first impression as I held this manuscript in my hand was that it was unusually *clean, fresh, and alive.* Our personal acquaintance with this author allows an insight into her motives and purpose for writing. That motive is pure and unpolluted by fame or finance.

Time demands allowed my wife, Judith, to read this book before I could do so. Judith's response, without edit or added commentary was, "After having read Sarah's book, the sense of *the manifest presence of the Lord* has increased in a way that I have long desired." A bit later, while encouraging me to do the reading, she said, "The last part is the most important. Sarah really does take you there."

Everyone knows that unsolicited commentary and recommendation is the most valuable and, for the most part, genuinely influential. My wife's commentary was influential and helpful as I personally entered this journey. The diligence, determination, and accuracy of each chapter and grouping spoke to me of pains–taking and time–consuming effort so that no one would be distracted or put off by carelessness or inaccuracy.

The one single, concentrated purpose, as you will discover, is to give us a *gift* of an uncommon insight into the skill of *abiding in the presence of God the Father*. Sarah has seen this. She has found the Pearl! She traded and sold all that was necessary for it to become her own. Eagerly, now, she seeks to present what she has seen so that we, too, can see and own this Pearl.

Pearl, in Scriptural thinking, is God's manifest presence. Principles, strangely enough, can continue to work and fascinate long after the presence has departed. This author will not permit that to happen. It simply is not possible to take this journey with her, incrementally and progressively, and not "get there"; our arrival being understood as a renewed sense and awareness of God's own manifest presence.

Each of us should allow this gentle and loving author to take us by the hand, instructing and guiding us into a greater awareness the Father's presence, seeking to make clear why this is happening. It is her gift to us. Receive it and act upon the instructions. A door or portal will open, allowing you to see and know the existential reality of a life lived in Father's presence.

It is our personal pleasure to be able to say, with integrity, that the question asked in the title question: *Are We There Yet?* has been actually and truthfully answered. We all would do well to receive this gift as one originating from the Lord's own hand and presented to us by the person of Sarah Ramsey.

—Bob and Judith Mumford
International Bible teacher and author

Introduction

The changing world around us has stirred within us as individuals the desire for a place of safety—a secure place. The fear of terror has caused our hearts to seek refuge.

- We can seek to protect ourselves.
- We can seek to be protected by government armies, Medicare, the Peace Corps etc.

or

- We can seek God and find His protection.

God wants to protect us. And when we seek His protection, we find more than we bargained for. We find shelter, peace, and protection! The Father has a secret place, a place of ultimate protection and peace, the place where God's presence dwells!

God has not only provided the secret place, but He gives us clear instructions how to arrive there. This study will show how to arrive at and abide in the secret place of the most high God. The secret things belong to the Lord. Daniel said, "I have a God who reveals secrets!" Daniel's God is my God too! Hallelujah.

God has secrets He wants us to know. God wants you to know:

- What the secret place is
- Where the secret place is located
- How to get to the secret place and dwell there.

Do you know the way into the secret place—the Holy of Holies? Our Father God wants you there. The Father has issued the invitation. He has made the way. He has provided a guide—a Helper to get us safely there—into His presence.

God's secret place provides for those who desire His provision. Where is God's secret place? How do I get there? These are the questions that will be answered as we make our journey through the tabernacle of Moses. The promises are great. God wants us to know the way. He has given us the pattern to come into his presence—the pattern of the tabernacle of Moses. The Christian life has a definite time of beginning, and it is a process that we walk through. It is a journey, a progressive journey.

God wants you there, in the secret place, in His presence. He has made every provision to assure your arrival. The invitation is clear—first to *draw near:* "Let us therefore come boldly to the throne of grace, that we may obtain mercy and find grace to help in time of need" (Hebrews 4:16). And to *enter into* the holiest of all: "Therefore brethren, having boldness to enter the holiest by the blood of Jesus, by a new and living way which He consecrated for us, through the veil, that is His flesh" (Hebrew 10:19). Let's learn to follow the pattern and draw near and enter into the presence of the Lord!

It is worth seeking. We are not on a wild goose chase. God's promise is, "seek and you will find" (Luke 11:9, NKJV) We are going to learn how to draw near to God. God is our Father, and He is a wonderful provider. He has made all the provisions for us to draw near to Him and dwell in His presence.

Many times we settle for far less than He has provided. We stop at the gate instead of entering in and being *with* Him. We settle for our sins being forgiven and the promise of eternal life when God has provided and desires a personal, intimate relationship. That's the reason He cleanses our sin—to bring us near to Him.

In this study we will find and follow the pattern God has provided for us in the tabernacle of Moses that takes us through the gate who is Jesus, into His courts and on into the holy place and the holy of holies, the secret place of the most high God.

> He who dwells in the secret place of the Most High shall abide under the shadow of the Almighty.
>
> (Psalm 91:1)

It is here in the secret place—above the ark of the covenant (which holds the rod, the manna, and the law), covered with the solid gold mercy seat, and surrounded by the wings of the two cherubim—that the Shekinah glory, the presence of God, came to dwell among the children of Israel.

Hebrews 8–9 tells us that the tabernacle of Moses is the pattern to follow to access the living presence of God today! Derek Prince has said that the pattern of the tabernacle of Moses is simple enough for a twelve-year-old child to follow. How wonderful!

Access into God's presence:

- The God of the ages
- God of the universe
- Almighty God!

God has made Himself accessible and has given us the pattern to follow that will lead us to Him. This book is about God's plan for man, who cut himself off from God's presence, to once again enter the presence of a holy God and to have fellowship with Him.

It is God's idea and plan to have man in His presence, and God has made complete provision to make it happen according to His plan. Our God is a seeking God:

- He seeks and saves those who are lost

- He seeks worshippers to worship Him in Spirit and in truth

- He seeks intercessors to bring others to Him

God created man in His image, and we are to be a seeking people. When we seek God with our whole hearts, we find Him (Jeremiah 29:13).

God wants to reveal Himself to man. He gave Jesus and Holy Spirit to show us the way. In John 14:6, Jesus said, "I am the way to the Father."

During the next twelve chapters, we will explore the pattern God gave Moses to reveal the way into the holiest of all, the place God chose to dwell among his people, Israel. The tabernacle of Moses reveals the pattern into God's presence. When we receive Jesus as our Savior, we are born again as babes, but we are to mature into sons. Growing in God is a process, and it requires pursuing and pressing into his plan. That is what we will do as we follow the pattern set before us in the tabernacle of Moses.

Where are we going? We are coming into the presence of the King of Glory, the King of kings, and Lord of lords! How awesome to have access to God almighty.

Just like Adam and Eve, we have an enemy who is continually luring us to come away from God and stop our journey.

The enemy

- Tells us it is not possible to finish
- Discourages us, and we lose hope
- Tells us it is too dangerous and fear grabs us
- Tells us there is no need for this journey

Pride tells us we are satisfied—
we don't need to pursue God.

We become interested in the things with which the enemy lures us—TV; sports; sex; money; our jobs; or other people, even our families, mates, or children; or the lure of a relationship that promises fellowship and satisfaction. We get our eyes off our goal, and we stop the journey before we reach the destination.

We become impatient and think, I will never get there. There probably isn't a secret place—a place of God's presence—or if there is, it is not until heaven that I can know God's presence. We think, I'm not holy enough for God's presence. And we ask, "Are we there yet? Are we there yet? Are we there yet?"

We become distracted with other things along the way and get on another road until we "come to ourselves" and remember where we are going.

- We remember our first love.

- We remember the peace.

- We remember the fellowship.

And we return, repent, and get back on the road to our destination! Doubt, discouragement, and unbelief will lure us away *if* we have not determined to finish and *if* we don't know where we are going.

It is not riches (prosperity) I am after... It is not healing... It is not any *thing... It is Him—Jesus, the Lord of glory!*

On this journey into the Father's presence, I am after Jesus. I am pressing into Jesus. I am in pursuit of the King, who has a kingdom. I want to be in His chambers, the place He dwells, the secret place.

Many of the distractions are not wrong in themselves or sinful, but they draw us away from our goal—the one thing we are seeking.

- The good things often keep us from the best

- The good things are distracting

- The good things get our attention away from our destination

We begin gazing on the things and lose the focus of our destination. Jesus is the way to the Father!

Like any journey, there will be times you may wonder if we will ever get "there." There are blessings at each of the stops on our journey, and you may think, *O this has to be "it."* You just ask, "Are we there yet?" Some of the stops in our journey will be to a place you may have already been. Those revisits will cause good memories to rise, and you may learn a new thing or two, because the Word of God is a *revealer.* Some of the stops will take longer than others. But you will know when you are "there." Let's pursue the Lord together. Let us come boldly before the throne of grace and find grace and mercy to help.

I will not sleep until I find for the Lord a dwelling (Psalm 132).

Psalm 91

He who dwells in the secret place of the Most High
Shall abide under the shadow of the Almighty.
I will say of the Lord, "He is my refuge
and my fortress;
My God, In Him will I trust."
Surely He shall deliver you from the
snare of the fowler
And from the perilous pestilence.
He shall cover you with His feathers,
And under His wings you shall take refuge;
His truth shall be your shield and buckler.
You shall not be afraid of the terror by night,
Nor of the arrow that flies by day,
Nor of the pestilence that walks in darkness,
Nor of the destruction that lays waste at noonday.
A thousand may fall at your side,
And ten thousand at your right hand;
But it shall not come near you.
Only with your eyes shall you look,
And see the reward of the wicked.
Because you have made the Lord who is my refuge,
Even the Most High your dwelling place,

No evil shall befall you,
Nor shall any plague come near your dwelling;
For He shall give His angels charge over you,
To keep you in all your ways.
In their hands they shall bear you up,
Lest you dash your foot against a stone.
You shall tread upon the lion and the cobra,
The young lion and the serpent you
shall trample underfoot.
Because he has set his love upon Me,
Therefore I will deliver him;
I will set him on high,
Because he has known My name.
He shall call upon Me, and I will answer him;
I will be with him in trouble;
I will deliver him and honor him.
With long life I will satisfy him,
And show him My salvation.

CHAPTER 1

God Reveals His Plan—
an Invitation into the King's Presence

The God Who Reveals Secrets

To know a secret or to have a secret and to be able to give it away is a real thrill. When someone has found treasure or someone is having a baby or getting married, this is great news we want to share. To be able to pass that secret on is exciting, both to the one who is the teller of the secret and to the one who gets the news. God has secrets, and He reveals those secrets. Amos 3:7 tells us, "Surely the Lord GOD does nothing, unless He reveals His secrets to His servants the prophets." And in Daniel 2:22, 28 the Bible says, "There is a God in heaven who reveals secrets" (verse twenty–eight), and "He reveals deep and secret things" (verse twenty–two).

I feel like one who has found the answer to a secret or a great mystery. I have known for many years that God has a secret place, the one that the Psalmist tells us about in Psalm 91. But I did not know where it was or how to get there. How about you? Do you know God has a secret place? Do you know where the secret place of the Most High is? Do you know how to get there? God wants to lead us into His secret place. He is in His secret place, and He wants you to be with Him there.

I have found the secret place of God's presence, His dwelling place, and I want to show you how to get there too. It is not hard, but there is a "way"! Let's look at it together.

God has secrets that He wants to share. He wants us to find the secret place of the most high God and dwell there. God wants someone with whom He can share His secrets. How do I know? His Word tells me. "Surely the Lord GOD does nothing, unless He reveals His secrets to His servants the prophets" (Amos 3:7). God reveals His secrets. He reveals deep and secret things: "There is a God in heaven who reveals secrets."[1]

God Wants You to Know

Where do we start? How do we begin to discover the secret place? Coming into God's presence begins with a hunger, a desire to be close to Him. I believe you *are* hungry or you wouldn't have chosen this book. When we have a holy reverence for God, He opens up His heart to us. "The secret of the LORD is with those who fear Him, and He will show them His covenant" (Psalm 25:14).

Did you know God wants you to know His secrets? In Luke 8:10 Jesus said, "To you it has been given to know the mysteries (*secrets of hidden truths*) of the kingdom of God."[2] God wants you to know His mysteries. One of those mysteries God wants to reveal is the way into His presence. He wants us to know the way into His secret place.

The Beginning

The Bible is a love story—the original love story—of a devoted Father desiring to have His children in His presence. It has always been God's plan to have His children in His presence. God's desire has always been to have fellowship with man. When He created Adam and Eve, He walked with them in the cool of the evening, and they enjoyed His presence.

How did man get separated from God in the first place? It was disobedience to God's Word. When Adam and Eve chose to heed the voice of Satan and disobey God, they cut themselves off from God's presence (Genesis 3). Their sin resulted in keeping God from dwelling among mankind. This broke God's heart but it did not stop God. *God had a plan.*

By choosing to be disobedient, man separated himself from God's presence. But through one man, Abraham, God began a nation by which He would restore His fellowship with man. Years later He raised up another man, Moses, to deliver that nation, the children of Israel, from Egypt. God gave Moses the plan that would provide the way that He would dwell with His people once again. In the old covenant, it was the tabernacle of Moses that provided God with a dwelling place in Israel among His people. *God's plan provided for man to make another choice, and that choice would restore his relationship with God.*

God's Plan for You

God knows and declares the end of a thing before He begins it. He knows how your life will end. He knows your end from your beginning. He has a plan for you. He sees you. He is El Roi, the "God who sees." One of the first ways God revealed Himself was in Genesis 16:13: God as El Roi, the "All–seeing God."

One place God describes His intimate knowledge of how He saw you before He formed you is in Psalm 139. In verse sixteen He says, "Your eyes [God's eyes] saw my substance, being yet unformed. And in Your book they all were written, the days fashioned for me, when as yet there were none of them." God knows the beginning, and He knows the ending. Jesus says, "I am the Alpha and the Omega, the Beginning and the End, the First and the Last" (Revelation 22:13). "Remember the former things of old, for I am God, and there is no other; I am God, and there is none like Me, declaring the end from the beginning, and from ancient times things that are not yet done, saying, 'My counsel shall stand, and I will do all My pleasure'" (Isaiah 46:9–10).

God has a plan to have you with Him. He has made every provision for you to dwell in His presence, not only in heaven, but as you live here on this earth. He has known you from the beginning, and He has a planned destination for you. Jeremiah 29:11 tells what His plan is for you—'"For I know the plans I have for you,' declares the LORD, 'plans to prosper you and not to harm you, plans to give you hope and a future.'"[3] Prosperity, safety, hope, and a future: this is God's plan for you. Your destiny—your destination—God has planned out for you. God's ultimate plan is to have you with Him, in His presence. He wants you to be with Him, and He has made all the provision to bring you to Himself. And when God's plans and purposes are fulfilled in your life, you are totally fulfilled!

Don't Lose Focus!

Sometimes our lives become so entangled in all that is happening around us that we lose focus of what we are doing or where we are headed. A few days ago in my morning prayer time, I was praying and reading the Bible and talking to God about all that was going in my life. I felt him say to me, "I know how to work it out." In my mind I saw a sewing box with threads all tangled together—such a mess that all I would have done was cut them off and throw them away. But I felt God say, "I know just which thread to pull to untangle the whole mess. It's not hard for me." Then in my mind's eye I saw a kaleidoscope. I felt the Lord say, "Just like a kaleidoscope, all those broken pieces in your life make a beautiful design when I am in charge." God knows how to put Humpty Dumpty together again!

God sees you. He has a plan, a plan of hope for your future, to prosper you and not to harm you. He has a destiny for you to fulfill. It's not hard for Him. He is God. He knows which thread to pull. He knows how to make the broken pieces beautiful.

We are exploring God's plan to have you in His presence. Why did God pay such a price for your salvation?

- To forgive your sin?

- To get you to heaven?

- To fill you with his Spirit?

Yes, all of these. But in John 14:6 Jesus said, "I am the way, the truth, and the life. No one comes to the Father except through Me." God gave us the gift of salvation *so that we can be with Him, and have fellowship with Him; to be with Him in His presence* and to make us holy so that we can come into His presence and dwell or abide there. Oh, yes! God wants me with Him in His presence!

Afraid of God's Presence

God gave the children of Israel the opportunity to come back into His presence, but fear kept them away (Exodus 19). God told Moses that those who kept His covenant would be a special treasure unto Him; they would be a holy nation and a kingdom of priests.

When the children of Israel had been out of Egypt and in the wilderness for three months, God called Moses up to the mountain. "And Moses went up to God, and the LORD called to him from the mountain, saying, 'Thus you shall say to the house of Jacob, and tell the children of Israel: "You have seen what I did to the Egyptians, and how I bore you on eagles' wings and brought you to Myself. Now therefore, if you will indeed obey My voice and keep My covenant, then you shall be a special treasure to Me above all people; for all the earth is Mine. And you shall be to Me a kingdom of priests and a holy nation." These are the words which you shall speak to the children of Israel'" (Exodus 19:3–6). God wanted a kingdom of priests.

The people agreed, but when Moses brought them out of the camp to the foot of the mountain to meet God, it was more than they could do. The presence of God was more than they could bear, and they drew back from Him. They were so afraid that they asked

Moses to just tell them what God was saying rather than go to Him themselves. So instead of having the kingdom of priests that He desired, God settled for Moses' brother, Aaron, to be a high priest to Him. Aaron and his sons were chosen to be priests under the old covenant.

The old covenant was not adequate. It was only the shadow of what was coming—but God's plan was fulfilled in Jesus in the new covenant.[4] Jesus came to be *the way* into the holy presence of God. When Jesus came, He fulfilled the demands of the Father's holiness, and the Father's desire was satisfied! When we receive Jesus, we become a priest unto God: "but you are a chosen generation, a royal priesthood, a holy nation, His own special people, that you may proclaim the praises of Him who called you out of darkness into His marvelous light" (1 Peter 2:9).

> Word Study: *Priest,* Hebrew kohen, *ko–hane;* Strong's #3548; lit. one *officiating,* a *priest;* also (by courtesy) an *acting priest* (although a layman):—chief ruler, X own, priest, prince, principal officer.[5]

Jesus gave to Father God the kingdom of priests that He had desired. As children of God, we have a purpose. Our purpose is to "proclaim the praises of Him" as priests offering sacrifices. John says in Revelation 1:5–6, "To Him who loved us and washed us from our sins in His own blood and made us kings and priests to His God and Father, to Him be glory and dominion forever and ever. Amen." We are a kingdom of priests created to offer sacrifices of praise to our God. Jesus gave the Father what He had desired, a kingdom of priests. Jesus is the way to the Father. God's plan makes provision for man to dwell once more in His presence as a kingdom of priests, a royal priesthood. As children of God we have a purpose—to "proclaim the praises of Him," as priests offering sacrifices.[6] We are to offer sacrifices of worship. We approach our God regarding Him as holy[7], with confidence, and we are to know Him as He desires—intimately, in His presence, dwelling in the secret place He has provided.

Make Me a Sanctuary

How could a holy God dwell in the midst of an unholy people? After Moses led the children of Israel out of Egypt, God called Moses up to the mountain and revealed the way He would once again dwell in the midst of His people. God's heart's desire has always been to dwell among His people. God's plan would fulfill His desire to dwell with man once again. A dwelling place was needed: "Let them make me a sanctuary, that I may dwell among them" (Exodus 25:8). God's dwelling place would be in the tabernacle of Moses, in the place called the Holy of Holies, above the ark of the covenant at the mercy seat. "And there I will meet with you, and I will speak with you from above the mercy seat, from between the two cherubim which are on the ark of the Testimony" (Exodus 25:22). Here the presence of the Lord would rest, and man could once again come into God's presence.

Determining the Value of God's Presence

Why should I want to know how to find God's presence? What is the value of the presence of the Lord?

> Word Study: *Presence,* Hebrew *paneh, (paw–neh)*; Strong's #6440; the *face* (as the part that *turns*);[8] in God's presence, in His face!

Moses, David, and Daniel were three men who knew the value of having the presence of God. When we know and value God's presence, we desire to be there.

Moses knew the value of God's presence, and what God told and showed Moses will help us. God revealed to Moses his plan to provide a dwelling place for God's presence, and we read in Exodus 25:21–22,

> You shall put the mercy seat on top of the ark, and in the ark you shall put the Testimony that I will give you. And there I will meet with you, and I will speak with you from above the mercy seat, from between the two cherubim which are on the ark of the Testimony, about everything

which I will give you in commandment to the children of Israel.

Okay, there it is: "at the mercy seat I will meet with you," God said, "and I will speak with you about everything."

When I saw this verse, my seeking began. *I want to meet with God. I want God to speak to me,* I thought. Where is the mercy seat, I wanted to know. I had been a Christian since I was eight years old; now I was fifty years old, and I didn't know where the mercy seat was or how to get there, but I desired to meet with God and to speak with Him and be in His presence. Moses valued the presence of the Lord. If God's presence did not go with him as he led Israel in the wilderness, Moses did not want to go. You know, I don't want to go without God's presence either, and I don't believe you want to go through life without the presence of God.

Moses had walked with God many years; he had led God's people out of Egypt and had been on the mountain with God and heard God's voice. And Moses had received the Law of God, written with the finger of God. Even after all these encounters with God, Moses's prayer in Exodus 33:13 was, "I pray, if I have found grace in Your sight, show me now Your way, that I may know You and that I may find grace in Your sight." God's answer was, "My Presence will go with you, and I will give you rest."

Then Moses said to God, "If Your Presence does not go with us, do not bring us up from here." Moses valued God's presence. I want God's presence with me too. Don't you?

David knew the value of God's presence. When David became king of Israel, his first priority was to return the ark to Israel, because God's presence dwelt there, above the mercy seat of the ark. In 2 Samuel 6:1–2, we read how David brought back "the ark of God, whose name is called by the Name, the LORD of hosts, who dwells between the cherubim." David knew where the presence of God dwelt, and when he became king of Israel he was determined to have the presence of God with him; he recovered the ark, which had been in the possession of the Philistines.

The presence of God dwelt in the tabernacle of Moses, in the holy of holies, between the cherubim, above the mercy seat, on top of the ark of the covenant. When David brought back the ark, he brought the presence of God back into Israel.

- It was the presence of God that gave Israel victory in their battles.

- It was the presence of God that gave them health.

- It was the presence of God that gave them prosperity.

- It was the presence of God that brought the blessing and glory of God.

- It was the presence of God that gave them rest and peace.

God's presence is valuable. David knew the value of God's presence. When you have the all–powerful, all–seeing, almighty God with you, on your side, you have all that you need. David said,

> Who is this King of glory?
> The Lord strong and mighty,
> The LORD mighty in battle.
> Who is this King of glory?
> The Lord of Hosts,
> He is the King of glory.[9]

The Lord mighty in battle—I don't know about you, but my battles have been so big and so hot that I need help! It is wonderful news to my ears that I can have the presence of the Lord—the Lord of hosts, the King of glory, the Lord mighty in battle—with me, on my side to help me.

David knew the value of God's presence.

> One thing I have desired of the LORD, that will I seek: that I may dwell in the house of the LORD all the days of my life, to behold the beauty of the LORD, and to inquire in His temple. For in the time of trouble He shall hide me in His pavil-

ion; in the secret place of His tabernacle He shall hide me; He shall set me high upon a rock.

Psalm 27:4–5

The presence of the Lord was so valuable to David that he had made it his number–one priority. He desired to dwell in God's presence. It was beautiful— he could inquire of the Lord, be hidden in the time of trouble, and be set high on a rock!

God wants me to know how to come into His presence. He is no respecter of persons. He has made full provision. He has given us the pattern into His presence. God has secrets, and He is the God who reveals them. God has a secret place. We see that in Psalm 91. He wants us to know how to find the secret place.

Daniel valued God's presence. In Daniel 2:20–22 Daniel blessed God before men, saying,

> Blessed be the name of God forever and ever, for wisdom and might are His. And He changes the times and the seasons; He removes kings and raises up kings; He gives wisdom to the wise and knowledge to those who have understanding. He reveals deep and secret things; He knows what is in the darkness, and light dwells with Him.

Even when Daniel was a young man

- he knew that God reveals deep and secret things
- he knew that it is God who changes times and seasons
- he knew that God gives wisdom and knowledge
- he knew God's presence—that light dwells in him and that He knows what is in the darkness
- he knew that God's wisdom and might removes and raises up kings

In verse twenty–eight he said, "There is a God in heaven who reveals secrets." Daniel knew the God who reveals secrets. You can know Daniel's God too!

God's Word reveals His secrets. (See Amos 3:7; Luke 8:10; Matthew 13:11.) The Word of God is my plumb line. I have learned not to rely on tradition, even though I love tradition. I have learned not to rely on what my denomination taught me. This is what I have learned to rely on: the Word of God. The Word of God is my standard. The Word of God is the truth, and truth is a person. As we read earlier, Jesus is the truth. I can put my whole weight, my whole faith, in the Word of God. Let every man be a liar, but God is always true. God's Word tells me that he does nothing without revealing his secrets to his servants, the prophets.[10]

How Does God Reveal His Secrets?

God wants us to know His secrets. Listen to what Paul said to the believers in Corinth: "But we speak the wisdom of God in a mystery, the hidden wisdom which God ordained before the ages for our glory, 'But as it is written: "Eye has not seen, nor ear heard, nor have entered into the heart of man the things which God has prepared for those who love Him." But God has revealed them to us through His Spirit. For the Spirit searches all things, yes, the deep things of God.'"[11]

How will God reveal His secrets? He will reveal them through His Spirit. The Holy Spirit, whom we received as a guarantee[12] of all God has for us, is our teacher, and the revealer of God's secrets. First Corinthians 2:12 says, "Now we have received, not the spirit of the world, but the Spirit who is from God, *that we might know* the things that have been freely given to us by God" (emphasis added). How will we know? The Holy Spirit is our teacher. We need to get to know Him. Jesus said in John 16:13, "When He, the Spirit of truth, has come, He will guide you into all truth." God desires to give us the spirit of wisdom and revelation. Paul prayed this prayer in Ephesians 1:17–18a: "I pray that the God of our Lord Jesus Christ, the Father of glory, may give to you the spirit of wisdom and revelation in the knowledge of Him, the eyes of your understanding being enlightened."

Open the eyes of my heart, Lord. I want to know Your secrets. Reveal to me the way.

God has revealed His plan for man to dwell in his presence in the pattern of the earthly sanctuary. The tabernacle of Moses was the pattern, shadow, or copy of the original in heaven.[13] The first covenant consisted of an earthly sanctuary: it was the pattern of heavenly things.[14] The tabernacle of Moses had three divisions: the outer court (or the courtyard), the holy place, and the holy of holies (or the holiest of all). The holiest of all was God's dwelling place, and under the old covenant only one man, the high priest, could enter, and only once a year on the Day of Atonement. Again, this was the result of man's choosing to draw back in fear.[15] This was not the "fear of God," but rather being afraid of God. There is a great difference in being afraid of and in having the fear of God.[16] The high priest, then, took the blood of a spotless lamb and offered it in worship as atonement for the sins of the children of Israel. This was a foreshadowing of Jesus, the spotless Lamb of God, whose blood would take away the sin of the world.

The New Covenant:
Jesus, the New and Living Way

When Jesus came and offered Himself as our sacrifice on the cross, His blood satisfied God's requirement once and for all. His blood cleanses us and blots out the sin and gives the believer access to God's presence. We can now come boldly into the presence of God just as the high priest did in the old covenant, but without restrictions! Oh, hallelujah, Jesus is the way! He has made the way into God's presence open for all who will accept Him. When Jesus died, the veil that separated man from God was taken away, and the holy of holies was opened.[17]

The old covenant showed us the pattern of things to come. The tabernacle of Moses is a pattern that shows us in the new covenant, the way Jesus brings us into the presence of God. God's dwelling place—the secret place of the most high God—opened by Jesus to man, satisfies both God and man! The secret place of the most high God is prepared for God's children. Psalm 91:1 says that we can dwell there: "He who dwells in the secret place of the Most High shall abide under the shadow of the Almighty."

Here God's desire is satisfied. God can once more meet and speak with man. The tabernacle would provide for the cleansing of sin that man needed. The tabernacle would provide what God required from man in order for him to come into the presence of the Lord. The tabernacle would provide God with a place to dwell and to be with man. The pattern of the tabernacle shows us as believers under the new covenant the way into the holiest of all—God satisfied, man satisfied! O Jesus! You did it!

The Dwelling

Where is the secret place? How do I get there? How may I dwell there? God wants to reveal His secrets. But treasures often require some digging! God's Word is full of treasures, "pearls" worth seeking.

The secret place of the most high God was the holiest of all in the tabernacle of Moses under the old covenant. Jesus has opened it for us, and the pattern of the tabernacle of Moses shows us how to enter in. As a believer I can learn the way, not just to visit, but by faith to abide in Christ and to dwell in His presence. I don't have to depend on another individual, my pastor, my church, prayer group leader, or a meeting or conference to get me into the presence of God. I can know how to access His presence myself. Isn't that awesome? *I have access to God*—to His presence by the blood of Jesus!

When I know how to access the presence of God, I can tell you and others how to also. It's God's provision. The pattern He gave Moses is fulfilled in Jesus Christ, our Lord. In Jesus Christ I have access to God! I come into His presence and worship Him.

"Here my heart is satisfied: within Your presence/ I sing beneath the shadow of Your wings"[18]—not in heaven, but now! Not only does God's plan satisfy *His* desire; it also satisfies my deepest need.

God's Invitation

God seeks worshippers. "But the hour is coming, and now is, when the true worshippers will worship the Father in spirit and truth; for the Father is seeking such to worship Him" (John 4:23). Man was made to worship God. What we worship is what has first place in our hearts. What we worship is what we think about and what we talk about; it is what we have on our minds. Man always worships something; when man worships God, through Jesus Christ, God's heart is satisfied. God seeks *me* to worship him! In worship, man's heart finds its desire and the purpose for his creation, and God is completely satisfied and the worshipper too is completely satisfied.

God is seeking worshippers, not only for the purpose of drawing near to Him, but to enter into his very presence. What Jesus ministers for us, as high priest, is the way into the presence of God. "For we do not have a High Priest who cannot sympathize with our weaknesses but was in all points tempted as we are yet without sin. Let us, therefore, come boldly to the throne of grace, that we may obtain mercy and find grace to help in time of need" (Hebrews 4:14–16). Let us draw near—but not *just* draw *near*—we can enter in! This is a journey! What we are looking for in this journey is to enter into the presence of God. We don't want to stop until we get there.

So the ball is in our court. Will we accept the invitation? Will we come to worship? Will we come to bow down? Will we come to say, "You're my God. You are altogether worthy, altogether lovely, altogether wonderful to me"?[19] What do you think? Do you want to take this trip? Do you want to journey into the presence of God? In the next chapters we will discover together the wonderful plan of provision, the pattern given in the tabernacle of Moses.

Let's count the cost and be faithful. We want to finish. "Better is the end of a thing than the beginning thereof" (Ecclesiastes 7:8). Luke 16:10 encourages us to be faithful in little: "He who is faithful in what is least is faithful also in much." So let us decide before we get started to finish and be faithful.

My Story

When I found the verse in Exodus 25:22 that at the mercy seat God would meet with me and talk with me; and when I found the promise in Hebrews 10:19 that by the blood of Jesus I could enter boldly into the holy of holies where the mercy seat is, I said, "Father, I don't understand very much, but I believe your Word; so I come boldly into your presence. I enter boldly into the holy of holies and to your mercy seat by the blood of Jesus." And as I in childlike faith began, God met me and began to teach me how to. Isn't that just like

Him? He takes the little mustard seed and begins to make it grow. I love you, Father God!

Will you draw near?
Let's begin to draw near. We have great promises to assure us that we are not on a wild goose chase. "Draw near to God and He will draw near to you" (James 4:8). God is moving toward us as we are moving toward Him. That will help us reach our destination much sooner.

"You will seek Me and find Me when you search for Me with all your heart. I will be found by you, says the LORD, and I will bring you back from your captivity" (Jeremiah 29:13–14a). Let your faith go. He wants to be found. Confess out loud, "Jesus, I am seeking you, and I will find you because I am searching for you with all my heart."

In the next chapter we will look at an overview of the tabernacle of Moses. Think of it as a brochure of your journey. We will look at the places we will go on this journey.

We will overview the three divisions of our journey and briefly look at the seven stops we will be making.

CHAPTER 2

Making God a Sanctuary—
a Brochure of the Journey

Man's Heart—Made for Fellowship with God

In the first chapter we saw how God reveals His secrets to His servants and that it is his desire for man to draw near to Him and enter in to fellowship with Him. God made man with a heart capable of fellowship with Him. He gave man a heart so great that nothing less than God could really satisfy it. Man needs personal, direct fellowship with God. God's Word reveals to us that our God is a God who reveals secrets and provides the way for man to come back into intimate fellowship with a Holy God through His Son, Jesus Christ. Jesus, as our high priest, made the way into God's presence open to all who will believe. Entering God's presence satisfies man's need to worship and God's desire for fellowship.

This chapter is an overview of the tabernacle of Moses, the pattern God gives to show us how to access His presence. In this chapter we will look at where this journey will take us. God has given us a pattern or map that leads us into His presence; this pattern is the tabernacle of Moses. Think of this chapter as the brochure of the journey or like a look from a hot air balloon ride that provides an overall view of the journey we are about to take. This chapter is full of information! The understanding will come as we visit each place; just like any journey you would make, you first look at the brochure, then when you go and visit each place, the experience becomes reality to you.

When my husband and I visited Israel in 2000, Israel came alive to us. This is my goal for you, that as you study the way into God's presence it becomes "life" to you.

The Pattern—How to Draw Near to God

What is the tabernacle of Moses? The tabernacle of Moses is the pattern of God's plan to dwell among the children of Israel under the old covenant. Jesus fulfilled the old covenant and gave us the new covenant in His blood that gives the one who believes in Him access into God's presence. The tabernacle of Moses is our map; it is the pattern that leads us into God's secret place, the holiest of all. In the new covenant, by following this pattern given to us in the tabernacle of Moses, we are led into the holiest of all—God's presence.

God often gives us patterns to help us. In the boxes below, you can see the pattern given to receive salvation, and the pattern Jesus gave to show us how to receive the Holy Spirit.

Pattern for Salvation

John 3:16

"For God so loved the world that He gave His only begotten Son, that whoever believes in Him should not perish but have everlasting life."

Here's the pattern:

1 . God loved

2 . God gave

3 . Man believes

4 . Man receives everlasting life

Pattern to Receive the Holy Spirit
John 7:37–39a

"Jesus stood and cried out, saying, 'If anyone thirsts, let him come to Me and drink. He who believes in me, as the Scripture has said, out of his heart will flow rivers of living water.' But this He spoke concerning the Spirit, whom those believing in Him would receive."

Here's the pattern:

1. Thirst

2. Come to Jesus—be born again

3. Drink—ask, be filled

4. Let the rivers flow!

The tabernacle of Moses is described in Hebrews chapter eight as a copy and shadow of heavenly things—made according to the "pattern." The tabernacle is the pattern that reveals the way into God's presence. This study of the tabernacle of Moses is the pattern, which when followed step by step in obedience will reveal how to draw near to God. Hebrews 8:5 reminds us what the Lord told Moses regarding the tabernacle, "See that you make all things according to the pattern shown you on the mountain." We know how to follow a recipe or a map or a pattern to get results. For instance, I have made gingerbread houses with my grandchildren. We follow a pattern. The pattern is not the real thing, but it shows us how to get what we want—a gingerbread house.

God has the pattern for the way into the presence of God. The tabernacle of Moses provides a map that can be followed and we can make a deliberate decision to come into God's presence as well as bring others also. Let's look at an overall view of the tabernacle before we begin our journey step by step.

The Tabernacle of Moses
What is the tabernacle of Moses?

> Definition: Tabernacle of Moses—a tent or dwelling place that was sacred, dedicated to God for His presence. It was sacred, dedicated because God would dwell there. He gave the Israelites and Moses in particular the pattern or precise plans for its construction.[20]

Because of God's desire to dwell among His people, he instructed Moses to direct the children of Israel to make a sanctuary for Him. A sanctuary is a sacred place. "And let them make me a sanctuary, that I may dwell among them. According to all that I show you, that is, the pattern of the tabernacle and the pattern of all its furnishings, just so you shall make it" (Exodus 25:8–9). The Hebrew word for sanctuary is shachan.

Word study:[21]

"That I may dwell" Hebrew *shachan* (*shah–chahn*) Strong's[22] #7931: To dwell, abide, remain, stay, tabernacle. This verb occurs more than 120 times. People *dwell* in tents (Ps. 120:5) or in a certain land (Jer. 7:7); God *dwells* in Mt. Zion (Is. 8:18); glory *dwells* in the Holy Land (Ps. 85:9). *Mishkan*, "tabernacle," God's "place of dwelling," is derived from *shachan*. This term also refers to the tabernacle of Moses and to other dwelling places as well. *Mishkan* occurs more than 50 times in Exodus alone. Another derivative of *shachan* is shekinah, the "abiding presence of Almighty God." Not found in Scripture, shekinah comes to us from Judaic writings. Sometimes the shekinah appears in a visible way.

Let's look at a diagram of the tabernacle—God's sanctuary.

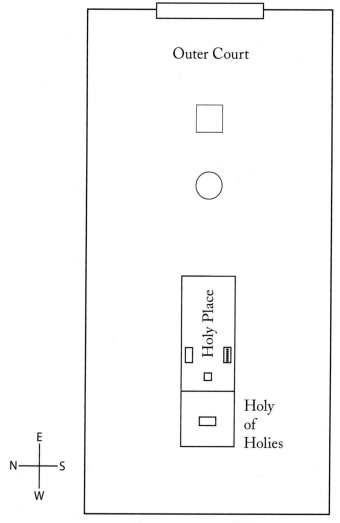

Diagram of the Tabernacle of Moses

Three Divisions—Three Progressive Steps toward God

Take a good look at the diagram and get familiar with the three divisions. A close look reveals three divisions:

- The outer court
- The holy place
- The holy of holies

These three divisions represent three successive or progressive steps in drawing near to God. They are progressive steps to entering into the presence of God. Every step brings the worshipper nearer—coming into maturity, perfection—pressing into God's presence.[23] "Your relationship with God is progressive, continually ascending to higher heights."[24] Have you found that your relationship with God is a process? We learn precept upon precept. As soon as you receive Jesus into your heart, you are invited to come near to God, to come boldly into His presence. Jesus's blood gives access to God! When God brings us into His presence, we often don't know how we got there, and we don't know how to come again by ourselves. But God wants us to know, and we are learning!

The tabernacle is a triune structure. Triune means three in one. It had three areas, three separate divisions,[25] making it one structure with three areas.

- The first area—the outer court (Exodus 27:9–19, 38:9–20)

    The outer court is the area that surrounds the tabernacle; it is the courtyard of the tabernacle. The tabernacle sits in the outer court. It is surrounded by a fence that is seven and a half feet high, and the fence is made of fine linen. The outer court has two pieces of furniture: the brazen altar and the brazen laver.

The outer court was one hundred fifty feet long and seventy–five feet wide, enclosed by a fine–twined linen curtain seven and a half feet high. The gate into the outer court was located on the east side of the court and was thirty feet wide. In the outer court was the structure of the tabernacle proper—fifteen feet wide and forty–five feet long (Hebrews 9:1–3, Exodus 26:33). It was divided into two sections. In the outer court, sin is dealt with and cleansing provided.

- The second area—the holy place (Exodus 26:33)

    The holy place is the first division of the tabernacle. There is also only one entry, and there are three pieces of furniture in the holy place. They are the golden lampstand, the golden table of showbread, and the golden altar.

The holy place, fifteen feet wide and thirty feet long, was the first division in the tabernacle proper.

The holy place is illuminated by the golden lampstand, and illumination is provided to finish the journey.

- The third area—the Holy of Holies (Exodus 26:33)
  The Holy of Holies is the third division of the tabernacle. This is our destination. God made the Holy of Holies His dwelling. The Holy of Holies was fifteen feet square. It was the second division in the tabernacle proper and was separated from the holy place by a heavy veil; it houses the ark of the covenant and the mercy seat. In the Holy of Holies, God is revealed.

Can you identify the three divisions? Do you see that the first division, the outer court, surrounds the tabernacle building and gives it a "courtyard" in which to sit? Can you see the tabernacle sitting in the outer court and see that it has two divisions? Can you picture it in your mind that it is about half the size of a football field? It is a copy and shadow of heavenly things! As we learn to see the three progressions in the tabernacle, it will give us understanding about the way we grow in Christ.

The Tabernacle Has Three Kinds of Light
Each division of the tabernacle has a different type of light. This is a distinguishing characteristic of each division and gives understanding to each area. If we understand the type of light available in each area, an

obvious distinction will be noted. Now there is no covering over the outer court, but the tabernacle building is covered. So think for a minute about the light. Outer court needs no light. The tabernacle gets no outside, natural light.

- Outer court—natural light: no covering (gets light from sun, moon, stars)
- Holy place—no natural light, completely covered (gets light from the golden lampstand)
- Holy of holies—no natural light, completely covered (is lit by the shekinah presence of God; the light of His presence)

The outer court is the largest division[26] and is the courtyard for the tabernacle. It had no covering and was lit naturally with the sun by day and the moon and stars by night. There was no natural light in the holy place or the Holy of Holies; very little light was in either because the tabernacle had four successive coverings. The coverings made the tabernacle a very dense structure, making it nearly impossible for any light to filter in.

The holy place, the second largest division,[27] had no natural light. It was covered with four successive coverings so little or no light could enter. We will learn that the only source of light was the seven-branched golden lampstand. Its lamps were filled with pure olive oil. The olive oil with a wick, burning like a candle, provided the light in the holy place. The oil in the lampstand is a type of the Holy Spirit. The lampstand illuminated the holy place.

When we come into the holy place, we get acquainted with the Holy Spirit. This may be compared to revealed truth: the truth of the Scripture revealed to the mind by the Holy Spirit. Before we know the Holy Spirit, the Word of God is often just black ink on white paper.

The holy of holies was the smallest division[28] and had the same covering as the holy place. Inside the holy of holies, there is no light—not even the light of the lampstand, because a heavy veil separated the holy place from the holy of holies. It was completely dark until the very presence of God Himself came in to illuminate it. Remember, the word *shekinah* is a word that comes from the Hebrew word meaning "to dwell." It means the manifest, indwelling presence of Almighty God in the midst of his people. The light of God's presence illuminates the holy of holies.

A Closer Look at the Three Divisions

Using the diagram on page 53 as a reference, let's take a closer look at the three divisions of the tabernacle. The whole outer court was enclosed, surrounded by a fence 100 cubits long and 50 cubits wide.[29] [One cubit is equal to one and a half feet, so the outer court, or enclosed area, was about 150 feet long and 75 feet wide (a football field is 100 yards, or 300 feet, long.)] This fence was made of pure linen. The linen curtains became a fence that made the triune tabernacle a unit.

The fence was five cubits, or seven and a half feet, high, so there was no way to take a peek at the courtyard from the outside. If you want to know what is inside, you must go in! *Many people want to know what it would be like to be saved before they get saved, but God has "made the fence too high to peep over." You have to commit yourself and walk in, so to speak, before God will show you what He has in store for you. This is a picture of how we have to be in Christ to be a partaker of the riches of God's grace.*[30]

There was no covering over the outer court. Remember it was exposed to the elements. The outer court had natural light from the sun, moon, and stars. This is a picture of how our natural minds perceive the things of God. But there comes a time when we must turn away from the natural and pursue the spiritual.

The holy place and the holy of holies were covered (Exodus 26:1–14). Little or no light could filter into the tabernacle. It was covered with four successive coverings, starting from the inside and working to the outside. This is the way God works within us too. God always begins his work on the inside and moves progressively to the outside.

When we come out of the outer court, we pass through the second veil into the holy place. It is the Holy Spirit that draws us into the holy place. We must have the light—the illumination—of the Holy Spirit to lead us into God's presence, the holiest of all, the secret place of the Most High. God sent the Helper to guide us into His presence.

We have seen this triune structure, the tabernacle of Moses, has three divisions and three kinds of light. Now let's look at the three entrances. The entrances show us how to get in!

The Three Entrances
Each division of the tabernacle had its own entrance.

- The outer court—the heavily embroidered linen gate into the outer court (Exodus 27:16).

- The holy place—the veiled door, also embroidered linen, into the holy place (Exodus 26:36).

- The holy of holies—the embroidered linen veil between the holy place and the holy of holies (Exodus 26:33).

The veils prevented peeking into one area of division while you were still in another. You could not see into the holy place from the outer court, and you could not see into the holy of holies from the holy place.[31] Again, to find out what it is like inside, we have to go inside. The Holy Spirit will lead and guide us to the gate first, then through the veiled entrance of the holy place, then into the holy of holies.

The pattern reveals three divisions, three types of light, and three different entrances.

See if you can name the three divisions, the three kinds of light, and the difference in the entrances.

The Tabernacle Furniture

There are pieces of furniture in each division of the tabernacle. There are seven different articles of furniture in the three divisions of the tabernacle: two in the outer court, three in the holy place, and two in the holy of holies. Each article represents a different way that Jesus prepares us to come into the presence of God.

The first two items of furniture are located in the outer court.

- The brazen altar or the great altar of brass
- The brazen laver or the laver of brass

Next, in the holy place, are

- The golden lampstand
- The golden table of shewbread
- The golden altar

In the holy of holies there are two articles of furniture

- The ark of the covenant
- The mercy seat with the cherubim

We will visit each one and apply it to our walk as we make the journey into the secret place of God's presence. Let's take a closer look at each of the seven articles of furniture.

- The brazen altar
  Once through the gate, we are immediately confronted by the brazen altar. The brazen altar is the place of sacrifice. The old covenant of the Old Testament required the blood of bulls and goats to *cover sin.* Under the new covenant of the New Testament, it is the blood of the spotless Lamb of God, the Lord Jesus Christ, who gave Himself for us. Jesus's blood *blots out* our sin and allows us to come into God's presence.[32] The blood is God's cleansing agent.[33] We are redeemed here at the brazen altar, a type of the cross. Here Jesus redeems us out of darkness into his marvelous light.[34] Jesus's blood gives us access to God's presence. Hallelujah! The blood of bulls and goats only covered sin, and sin cannot come into God's presence—but the blood of Jesus blots out sin and allows us to come boldly before the throne of grace!

- The brazen laver

  Just beyond the brazen altar in the outer court is the brazen laver, a large brass pan full of water. The water is the second cleansing agent. The water represents the Word of God[35]. The blood and the water cleanse us and make us holy and prepare us to be filled with the Holy Spirit. In the outer court sin is terminated! The blood and the water cleanse the believer. (Can you see already a clean vessel ready to be filled?)

- The golden lampstand

  The golden lampstand in the holy place illuminates this area of the tabernacle. The light from the lampstand gives light and reveals the three articles of furniture in the holy place: the golden lampstand, the golden table of showbread, and the golden altar of incense.

- The golden table of showbread

  With light from the lampstand, we can see the way to the table of showbread where we eat the bread of His presence with other priests.

- The golden altar

  The light from the lampstand also reveals the golden altar where we worship Jesus and intercede for others.

- The golden ark of the covenant
  The golden ark of the covenant contains three items: the tablets of the law, Aaron's rod that budded, and the golden pot of manna.

- The mercy seat
  The solid gold mercy seat rests on top of the ark of the covenant.

Our destination on this journey is the mercy seat in the holy of holies. God said, "There I will meet with you, and I will speak with you from above the mercy seat, from between the two cherubim which are on the ark of the Testimony."[36] The mercy seat is the dwelling place of the most high God; it is the throne of grace.[37]

Review

As we enter the gate of the tabernacle, we find three distinct divisions: the outer court, the holy place, and the holy of holies. Each division has a different type of light and a distinct entrance.

Each step we take brings us closer to the secret place of the Most High, and with each progression, the light changes to reveal more of God's presence to us. The glory of the Lord filled the tabernacle, and the priests followed the glory.[38] We learn that the Holy Spirit draws us, and because we have been cleansed by the blood of the Lamb, we have boldness to enter in to the holy of holies. [39] We then come to the throne of grace, which is typified in the mercy seat atop the ark of the covenant—the secret place of His tabernacle (Psalm 24:5). I can feel the anticipation rising! At this point I just come running! Then I learn as I go! Proverbs 2:2 says, "Apply your heart to understanding." When I understand it gives great foundation to my experience!

The tabernacle, God's pattern given to Moses,[40] was a shadow of what was to come in Jesus.[41] This pattern gave the priests access into His presence, and this pattern is applicable today. Under the old covenant, only the sons of Aaron had access to the tabernacle, but since Jesus came and died and rose again, his blood gives all who come to Him access into the Father's presence. Jesus is the way to the Father; He is the Way, the Truth, and the Life. He takes us to the Father. Everything in the tabernacle reveals a facet of God—precise, detailed. The materials used, the sizes, dimensions, the colors, and how the positioning of the furniture imitates the shape of the cross, all point to a loving Father desiring to bring His people into His presence.

Are you looking forward to the journey? Can you see a glimpse of where we are going—the progression? I can't wait to take you. We are made to dwell in God's presence, and He has made every provision to make us clean and to give us the clothing we need to come into the presence of the Lord of glory!

Interesting Notes

- One interesting thing about the tabernacle is that the Holy of Holies was absolutely, exactly and geometrically in the center of God's people. They camped around the presence of God on all sides. "The Lord thy God in the midst of thee is mighty" (Zephaniah 3:17; See also Matthew 18:20).

- Another interesting note: if the people who camped around the tabernacle were drawing near to God, they were also drawing near *to one another*. The same is true for us today. If we draw near to God, we draw near to those that are drawing near!

- Remember, this is an overview of the tabernacle; we are just getting familiar with where we are going on this journey.

Our study will not be detailed but will be the pattern that shows us the way into the presence of God. We will not be going into much of the symbolism of the tabernacle, its construction or articles of furniture, but rather, our study will focus on learning "how to" enter into the holiest of all.

The Process of Preparing a People for God's Presence

Entering into God's presence is a *process*. As we look at the tabernacle of Moses, we will learn the pattern for entering God's presence. The whole process has the purpose of preparing a people for His presence. Since sin cannot dwell in God's presence, He has made the way of salvation to prepare us to come in, to draw near. "By those who come near Me I must be regarded as holy; and before all the people I must be glorified" (Leviticus 10:3).

In the coming chapters, we will examine in detail the progressive steps of our journey into the secret place of the most high God. We will stop at each piece of furniture, cooperate with the Holy Spirit, and as we yield ourselves to the Holy Spirit, He works in us and enables us to complete this journey. Looking again at our diagram, the first thing we come to as we begin our journey is the gate.[42] The gate is the entrance to the outer court and has natural light. There is only one way to enter, and that is through the gate. The gate is Jesus.[43] A fence of white linen—a wall, a curtain of righteousness—surrounds us. Jesus gives us *His* righteousness,[44] and it surrounds us. This is where the journey begins.

Do you see where we are going? To go on this journey is a personal decision. Have you made this decision? Have you already begun the journey? Have you recognized places where God has already brought you? Do you see places you want to go? This is a journey that will forever change your life and forever change how you relate to your heavenly Father. Have you decided to make this journey into the secret place of the most high God? You will never regret it. Make this personal decision to finish the journey.

Let's pray:

Thank you, Father, for Your love and for Your desire to draw me to Yourself. Jesus, You are the way to Father. I believe You are God's Son and that You died, were buried, and rose again the third day and that You are sitting at the right hand of your Father. Cleanse me of my sin and take me into God's presence.

Thank You for Your plan and for Your provision for Your children, for me to dwell in Your presence. Open my heart; reveal to me Your ways. Oh, God, teach me to walk in them. In Jesus's name, Amen.

CHAPTER 3

The Outer Court—the Brazen Altar—
Jesus the Terminator of Sin

In the first two chapters we became familiar with God's purpose to dwell among His people. We saw His plan to carry out that purpose both in the Old Testament through the provision of the sacrifices in the tabernacle of Moses and in the fulfillment of the old in Jesus Christ, who gave Himself on the cross and is the way to Father God. We saw the big picture, an overview of the tabernacle of Moses, and learned that the pattern of entering into the presence of God was shown through the different areas of the tabernacle:

- The white linen fence

- The gate

- The outer court, with the brazen altar and the brazen laver

- The holy place is entered through the veil; the golden lampstand, the golden table of showbread, and the golden altar are in the holy place.

- The holy of holies was separated from the holy place by a thick veil until Jesus died and the veil was torn in two. The holy of holies houses the ark of the covenant covered by the mercy seat.

In this chapter we visit the first stop in our journey, the brazen altar[45]. We cannot continue the journey without coming to the brazen altar, which is a picture of what Jesus did at the cross. In the old covenant, the brazen altar is the place of sacrifice for sin, the blood of bulls and goats. In the new covenant, Jesus is our spotless Lamb, our sacrifice, and the sacrifice for sin on the cross. The brazen altar in the old is symbolic for the cross of Jesus Christ in the new.

The tabernacle of Moses is a replica, a pattern, a shadow of the salvation offered through Jesus Christ, the Savior of the world. The tabernacle is a beautiful picture in the old covenant of what Jesus accomplished in the new covenant. Jesus fulfilled the old! The Tabernacle is a triune structure, surrounded by a linen curtain, which represents God's righteousness. The children of Israel came to the gate with a sacrifice, a lamb, a bird, etc., to be the atonement or payment for their sin. This is a picture or pattern of God's plan of salvation through Jesus, the spotless Lamb, who is the gateway into God's righteousness. The pattern of the tabernacle of Moses reveals how to come all the way into God's presence, one step at a time.

When you decide to come to Jesus and receive Him as your spotless Lamb, you have decided to make the journey. You've made the best choice of your life! Your soul will be satisfied in the presence of God.

The Starting Point of the Journey—the Gate

There is only one starting point in our journey into God's presence; there is only one way in, only one gate.

> Word Study: *Gate* Hebrew *sha'ar* (shah'–ar) Strong's #8179: an opening, i.e., door or gate. [46]

The journey begins at the gate, the entrance into the tabernacle: Jesus is the gate. Exodus 27:16 says, "For the gate of the court there shall be a screen twenty cubits long, woven of blue, purple, and scarlet thread, and fine woven linen, made by a weaver. It shall have four pillars and four sockets."

The linen curtain fence established the tabernacle boundary. Because it was seven and a half feet high, you could not see inside. The gate gave the *one point of entrance* into the tabernacle. There was only one entrance—not many entrances—one. *But* "whosoever will,"[47] may enter by the gate.

Moses was given the pattern to set up the court and hang the gate! Exodus 40:8 says, "You shall set up the court all around, and hang up the screen at the court gate."

We begin our journey by *entering* the gate. Jesus said in John 10:7, "I am the gate for the sheep." As we come to the gate today, the entrance of the tabernacle, we are not ignorant; we come with awareness that we are seeking God *His* way—one way, through Jesus Christ his Son. Jesus is our sacrifice—our Spotless Lamb. *O Lord, You are good! You provided the Lamb for us!* The worshipper comes through the gate with his sacrifice, and we come with the spotless Lamb of God, who is our sacrifice for sin.[48] Jesus became sin that we might receive His righteousness.[49] We come through the gate and inside the linen curtain, inside God's boundaries of righteousness surrounding our salvation.

The Outer Court

So, how do we access the presence of God? We accept Jesus as the sacrifice for our sin, and we come through the gate and enter the outer court. We are making our way to the holy of holies. We are now taking the first step of our journey into God's presence. We often get in the gate and make the first step of the journey and stop. Remember, we have a destination, and that is to be in the holy of holies, the secret place of the most high God. We want to be *in His presence*. Jesus is the way to the Father—lead on, Lord Jesus!

Entering through the gate brings us into the outer court. We come with our sacrifice, the spotless Lamb of God, the sacrifice for our sins, Jesus Christ. We are entering the courts of God, thankful that He dwells among His people and that He, as our spotless Lamb, has made provision, "the way," to enter into God's kingdom. As New Testament believers, our journey begins as we come to Jesus and enter the gate that brings us into His court. Most of us know the song taken from Psalm 100:4: "I will enter His gates with thanksgiving in my heart, I will enter His courts with praise." *This is that court!* The Psalm describes the manner in which we come into the courtyard. We enter His courts when we come through Jesus, the gate—thankful for Jesus, the way, into the outer court. Under the old covenant, when the worshipper came to the gate, he had to bring an offering, (sacrifice)[50] to enter in and worship. Thank you, Father, for providing for us the spotless Lamb of God, the perfect sacrifice.

The Brazen Altar

When we enter the gate and come within the linen curtain fence of the outer court, the first thing we see is the brazen altar. We have no choice but to come face to face with the altar. It is the largest piece of furniture in the Tabernacle and sits very conspicuously in the outer court. It dominates the entrance, being seven and a half feet square.

Let's look at the brazen altar. Its description is given in Exodus 27:1–8:

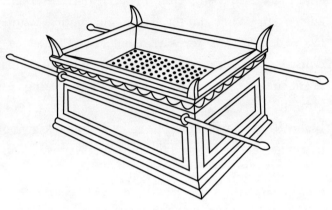

Brazen Altar

You shall make an altar of acacia wood, five cubits long and five cubits wide—the altar shall be square—and its height shall be three cubits. You shall make its horns on its four corners; its horns shall be of one piece with it. And you shall overlay it with bronze. Also you shall make its pans to receive its ashes, and its shovels and its basins and its forks and its firepans; you shall make all its utensils of bronze. You shall make a grate for it, a network of bronze; and on the network you shall make four bronze rings at its four corners. You shall put it under the rim of the altar beneath, that the network may be midway up the altar. And you shall make poles for the altar, poles of acacia wood, and overlay them with bronze. The poles shall be put in the rings, and the poles shall be on the two sides of the altar to bear it. You shall make it hollow with boards; as it was shown you on the mountain so shall they make it.

Moses made the brazen altar according to the pattern given by God—what attention to detail!

There are two articles of furniture in the outer court, the brazen altar and the brazen laver; both were made from brass, which is a type or picture of sin. The brazen altar was made of acacia wood overlaid with brass. It looks like gold, but is not—it tarnishes. It has been said that because all of its sides were covered with polished brass, the moment you walked inside and looked at it, you saw yourself in its reflection. You see yourself, the problem, and you see the altar, the solution to the problem.

> Word Study:[51] *altar, mizbeach* (meez–*beh*–ahch); Strong's #4196:[52] Altar, place of sacrifice. The root of *mizbeach* is *zabach,* which means "to slay, to sacrifice, to offer an animal." The word *mizbeach* occurs more than 400 times. Altars were of great importance in the lives of Noah and the three patriarchs. In the Levitical system and in Solomon's temple, the altar was the center of daily activity, without which the rest of Israel's worship could not take place. The "altar of sacrifice" was also crucial in God's revelation of true worship for joyful times, such as feasts.

So an altar is a place of sacrifice. This one was made of brass, representing sin. The brazen altar was the place where the sacrifice for sin was made. The blood of bulls and goats was offered on the brazen altar as atonement for the sin of the families of the children of Israel.

The Cross—the Place of Reckoning

The brazen altar is a type of the cross—it is where the blood of the sacrifice was spilled and the sacrifice consumed. When you come to God, the first thing that you encounter is the cross, and you see yourself mirrored in it. The cross is a place of reckoning. "Come now, and let us reason together," says the Lord, "Though your sins are like scarlet, they shall be as white as snow; though they are red like crimson, they shall be as wool" (Isaiah 1:18). Sin cannot enter God's presence. Until your sins are forgiven, there can be no further progress into God's presence; because God is holy and sin cannot enter His presence. At the brazen altar, the blood is received to deal with sin. *Sin keeps us from God. The blood gives us access to God.* There is no entry into all that God has for you if you bypass the cross. There is no other way in. God has provided for our sins to be forgiven through the death of Jesus on the cross. Jesus became sin that we might receive His righteousness.

It was here, at the brazen altar, that the Lamb was slain, and His blood poured out. It was here that the blood was exchanged for sin, for "without the shedding of blood, there is no remission" (Hebrews 9:22). Romans 6:23 says, "The wages of sin is death." Blood has to be shed as the penalty for sin. Leviticus 17:11 says, "For the life of the flesh is in the blood, and I have given it to you upon the altar to make atonement for your souls; for it is the blood that makes atonement for the soul."

Are we too familiar with the cross? Because we think we know about the cross of Jesus Christ, are we in danger of rushing past the altar? Our journey does not end at the brazen altar or at the cross, but we must enter with the sacrifice—there must be atonement for sin. The price for sin had to be paid. The blood was shed on the altar as the penalty for sin. The life is in the blood.

Atonement

What is atonement? In his book *Atonement*, Derek Prince says:

> Divide the word up in three syllables: *at–one–ment*. That is what atonement really means—that God and the sinner are brought into a relationship in which they are *at one*. In Hebrew the word is *kippur* and means "covering." The Day of Atonement was a day of *covering*. By the sacrifices offered on that day, the sins of the people were *covered*, but only for one year. The

picture in the New Testament is totally different... Hebrews 10:3–4 speaks of the sacrifices of the Old Testament: "In those sacrifices there is a reminder of sins every year." So, far from taking sin away, those sacrifices reminded the people of the problem of sin. "For it is not possible," the writer continues, "that the blood of bulls and goats could take away sins." In Hebrews 9:26, on the other hand, the writer speaks about what was accomplished by the death of Jesus, in direct contrast to the Old Testament sacrifices. In the second half of that verse, speaking of Jesus, the writer says: "But now, once at the end of the ages, He has appeared to put away sin by the sacrifice of Himself.'" So when Jesus came and offered Himself as a sacrifice on the cross, He *put away* sin. John the Baptist introduced Jesus in John 1:29, "Behold! The Lamb of God who takes away the sin of the world!" *Jesus took away sin.*[53]

That is atonement. Justified—just as though I never sinned! (Surely, that can't be true! That is way too good.) It is true! So atonement is my sin blotted out, put away, as far as the east is from the west. Do you know how far that is? If you start going east, you will never get to the west!

Just as with Adam and Eve, the fig leaves could not cover their sin. God covered them with the skin of an animal. Blood was shed and God provided. We too must have our sin dealt with. Our sin is against God, and God has made provision. Jesus has made atonement for our sin, *but* we must accept the blood of Jesus to cleanse our sin by faith! All this is here at the first stop in our journey. God made provision for sin in the old covenant at the brazen altar, and God makes provision for sin in the new covenant when we come to the cross and accept the great exchange of Jesus's death for the gift of His life. It is through the offering, Jesus giving his life's blood, that we receive His life.

The New and Living Way—the Cross is Central
As we just learned, in order for man to come into God's presence, sin must first be dealt with. Sin separates man from God, for God is holy, and sin cannot enter his presence. God provided a way in the old covenant, but the sacrifice of animals and the spilling of their blood as a sin offering were but a foreshadowing of what was to come in Jesus Christ, the Lamb of God. The blood of animals was not sufficient to satisfy the wrath of a holy God against sin.[54] Sin was only *covered* by the sacrifice of bulls and goats, but the people of Israel, in faith, believing that God would send a Redeemer, carried out the plan set forth in the old covenant.

So in his great love for man, God made provision through the death of his own Son as our sin offering. He made provision to clean us up—to make us holy. He cleanses us and provides salvation. This is God's idea. He wants us with him! This is the new and living way.[55] The blood of Jesus forever *blots out* our sin, and it will never more be remembered![56] The whole process is required by God, because he is holy. *To approach a holy God, we must be holy.* Leviticus 11:45 states, "For I am the LORD who brings you up out of the land of Egypt, to be your God. You shall therefore be holy, for I am holy." When I saw that I must be holy, I always thought that could not happen! Now I see that He makes me holy; His blood cleanses; He has made provision for holiness (Hebrews 13:9).

At the moment Jesus gave up his life, the way into the holy of holies was opened.[57] Hallelujah! The mystery of what Jesus meant when He said, "It is finished," is revealed here at the brazen altar. His death was like the lamb being slain by the priests in the old covenant, its blood spilling over the altar as a sin sacrifice. Jesus took his own blood (not the blood of bulls and goats) into heaven and placed it on the mercy seat to atone for our sin! When we come to and accept the cross of Christ, when we believe in our hearts and confess with our mouths that Jesus is Lord, and that God has raised Him from the dead, we have made the first stop on our journey.

It is at the cross, represented in the tabernacle of Moses by the brazen altar, where a spotless lamb was sacrificed and the blood was given for forgiveness of sin. This blood was sprinkled on every piece of furniture in the tabernacle.[58]

Our stop at the cross, the brazen altar, gives us access to complete the rest of the journey because we have the blood. It was provided for us, and it gave holiness both to the worshipper and to the articles of furniture in the tabernacle. *God is cleaning me up,* getting me ready for his presence. The blood of Jesus cleanses me from all sin as I walk in God's light.[59] The blood of Jesus sprinkles my conscience, and I come boldly into God's presence. It is the blood of Jesus that gives me access to God.

Jesus, the Redeemer

What does it mean to be redeemed? When we go to the grocery store with a coupon valued at one dollar, and we give it to the cashier, we redeem that coupon. We are of high value to our heavenly Father, and He has paid the price to redeem us from sin with His own precious blood. He has made provision to buy us back!

Let's take some time here and examine what the Word has to say about this redemption in Christ Jesus.

> Word Study:[60] *Redemption, apolutrosis* (ap–ol–oo–tro–sis); Strong's #629: A release secured by the payment of a ransom, deliverance, setting free. The word in secular Greek described a

conqueror releasing prisoners, a master ransoming a slave, and redemption from an alien yoke. In the New Testament it designates deliverance through Christ from evil and the penalty of sin. The price paid to purchase that liberation was his shed blood.

Romans 3:23–25 (NLT) says,

For all have sinned and fall short of the glory of God, and are justified freely by His grace through *the redemption* that came by Christ Jesus. God presented Him as a sacrifice of atonement, through faith in His blood. He did this to demonstrate His justice, because in His forbearance He had left the sins committed beforehand unpunished.

(emphasis added)

God has made provision for sin, paid our price, our penalty. This happened when Jesus gave his life and shed His blood on the cross. We accept God's provision when we believe in Jesus's death by faith. Jesus secured our deliverance from sin and paid the price to free us from sin!

Our Wonderful Redeemer—

- Justified—We have been justified by His blood just as though we had never sinned (Romans 5:9).

- Redeemed—We have redemption through His blood (Colossians 1:14 and Ephesians 1:7).

- Cleansed—We have cleansing through His blood (1 John 1:7).

(Make it a priority to memorize these verses)

Let's just stop and thank the Father for the blood of Jesus. The Father never tires of hearing us declare what the blood of Jesus means to us. The Word of God tells us that a thousand years is as a day to God and a day is as a thousand years.[61] Even though it has been two thousand years since Jesus sacrificed his blood and gave his life, to the Father it is only as if two days have passed.

Thank You, Father, for the blood of Jesus that justifies me just as though I have never sinned, that redeems me and lets me come near You. Thank You for the blood of Jesus that gives me forgiveness of sins and cleanses me from all unrighteousness. Jesus is listening for your confession. Did you say it out loud with your mouth?

Restating Hebrews 9:26, the same truth, Jesus came to put away sin by the sacrifice of Himself. "Then Christ would have had to suffer many times since the creation of the world. But now He has appeared once for all at the end of the ages to do away with sin by the sacrifice of Himself." This speaks of Christ, emphasizing that He only suffered once; when He did it once, it was complete, finished. He didn't need to do it again as the priests had to do in the old covenant with the blood of animals. Jesus did everything that ever needed to be done! Did you know that when you get to heaven you won't be any more born again than you are right now? Jesus finished the work of salvation, and when we believe, we receive His finished work! It's almost too good to be true! But it is true. It is the truth!

The Great Exchange—
God's Extravagant Provision

Second Corinthians 5:21 states, "God made Him [Jesus] who had no sin to be sin for us, so that in Him [Christ] we might become the righteousness of God." (emphasis added) There's the exchange: He was made sin with our sinfulness that in return we might be made righteous with His righteousness. His blood takes away, *blots out, sin*—my sin. Jesus's blood does not cover my sin; Jesus's blood blots out my sin![62] God is cleaning up sin in me so I can come and be with Him. He is holy; He cleanses me and makes me holy!

- Jesus was punished that I might be forgiven—Isaiah 53:4–5; Colossians 1:19–22

- Jesus was wounded that I might be healed—Isaiah 53:4–5; 1 Peter 2:21

- Jesus was made sin with my sinfulness that I might be made righteous with His righteousness—Isaiah 53:10; 2 Corinthians 5:21

- Jesus died our death that we might share His life—John 10:10; Romans 6:23

- Jesus was made a curse in that we might receive the blessing—Galatians 3:13–14

- Jesus endured my poverty that I might share His abundance—2 Corinthians 8:9

- Jesus endured our shame that we in turn might have His acceptance—Isaiah 53:3; Ephesians 3:1–6

- Jesus made me a new man in Christ—Romans 6:6–7; 1 Corinthians 5:17[63]

We can feel the presence of God here at the brazen altar as the great exchange is made: our sin for the righteousness of Jesus, our condemnation for His justification. This is the first stop on our journey into the presence of God.

Here at the cross our salvation is complete. In a very real sense we are on our way home. We have all we need to complete the journey, *but the cross is not the destination; rather, it is the beginning. Our destination is not the brazen laver in the outer court, but the mercy seat in the holy of holies.* Jesus is the Way, the Truth, and the Life; He takes us to the Father.

Are we there yet?

We are learning how to draw near to God, but the journey is not complete with just one stop. It is progressive. We are not just trying to escape hell and make heaven our home. We want to know how to love and be pleasing to God. We want to dwell in His presence *now* while we are living on earth. When we read Psalm 91 and see the blessings for the one who dwells in the secret place of the Most High, we desire to know how to dwell in the secret place.

When God works, he moves from the inside out. We are going from the outside in. In the book of Exodus, God gave the plan of the tabernacle, starting with the ark and the mercy seat and moving outward.[64] The initiative in salvation, in redemption, is from God and not from man. God always draws man and moves toward man. We are not the initiator. You will find in the unfolding of the tabernacle that we are going on our journey in the opposite direction than that Scripture showed. This is deliberate. The purpose is to show the work of Jesus from beginning to end. Because we have the completed Word, we can come this way. Just remember that if God had not been willing, none of this would have happened. Jesus was our sacrifice and without His going to the cross for us there would have been no salvation. We must have our sin forgiven—our old nature crucified—if we are to dwell in God's presence. To dwell in God's presence is the destination of our journey.

Are we there yet? No, we have only entered and made the first stop. But we cannot make the journey into the presence of God without stopping at the brazen altar, the shadow/copy of what God would do when He shed the blood of Jesus, the spotless Lamb on the cross of Calvary!

When we have the blood of Jesus, we have what we need to access the presence of God. Let us enter boldly with our consciences sprinkled.[65] This is not a long journey if we won't get distracted (lured away by our own lusts). We must first come to the cross! Don't let familiarity—what you already know—keep you from the lavish love of the cross of Christ! The passion of Christ opened the holiest!

Before Continuing

"Have you been to Jesus for the cleansing power? Are you washed in the blood of the Lamb?"[66] We have established that the brazen altar must be our first stop, and that it represents the cross of Jesus Christ. Have you come to the cross and received forgiveness of sins as shown in Romans 10:8–10?

> The word is near you, in your mouth and in your heart (that is, the word of faith that we preach): that if you confess with your mouth the Lord Jesus and *believe* in your heart that God has

raised Him from the dead, you will be saved. For with the heart one believes unto righteousness, and with the mouth confession is made unto salvation.

Have you believed in your heart that Jesus has been raised from the dead? Have you confessed with your mouth that Jesus is Lord? If not, you can ask Jesus right now to cleanse you. Confess what you believe. Once you have asked Jesus to cleanse you from sin, spend time thanking Jesus for His blood and for what His blood has accomplished.

After coming to the cross (entering by the gate) and receiving Jesus, we are ready to go on. Can you believe there is more—more than those great exchanges? This is only the first stop. We are destined for the throne—to be seated with God, to be in his presence.[67] Jesus is the way to the Father. We are now ready to visit the second piece of furniture in the outer court, the brazen laver, as we make our way toward the holiest of all.

Let's pray, let's enter into his courts with thanksgiving:

Thank You, Father, for wanting me with You.
Thank You for Your plan to blot out my sin.
Thank You, Father, for Jesus.
Thank You, Jesus, for becoming my sacrifice, giving life,
Your blood, to cleanse me and make me holy.
Thank You, Father, that the blood of Jesus justifies me just
as if I had never sinned.

Thank You, Jesus, that You were punished that I might be forgiven.

Thank You, Jesus, that You were wounded that I might be healed.

Thank You, Jesus, that You were made sin with my sinfulness that I might be made righteous with Your righteousness—thank You, Jesus, for making me righteous.

Thank You, Jesus, for dying my death that I might share Your life.

Thank You, Jesus, for giving me Your life.

Thank You, Jesus, for becoming the curse that I might receive the blessing.

Thank You, Jesus, for enduring my poverty that I might share Your abundance.

Thank You, Jesus, for Your abundance.

Thank You, Jesus, for bearing my shame that I might share Your glory.

Thank You, Jesus, for enduring my rejection that I might have Your acceptance.

Thank You, Jesus, that I am crucified with Christ and alive to God.

Thank You, Jesus, that I can come boldly into Your presence with my conscience sprinkled clean by the blood of Jesus.

Jesus, I come.

Draw me close to You, Jesus.

Take me to the Father. Amen.

CHAPTER 4

The Outer Court—the Brazen Laver—Jesus the Word of God

The first stop on our journey into the holy of holies is the brazen altar; it is symbolic of the cross. The brazen laver, the second piece of furniture in the outer court of the tabernacle and the second stop on our journey, is symbolic of Jesus, the Word of God. Father God provides for His children to be clean inside and outside! At this point, we are still in the outer court. Having applied the blood of Jesus at the cross, which the brazen altar pictures, we are now ready to be washed by the pure water of his Word.

Exodus 30:17–21:

> Then the LORD spoke to Moses, saying: "You shall also make a laver of bronze, with its base also of bronze, for washing. You shall put it between the tabernacle of meeting and the altar. And you shall put water in it, for Aaron and his sons shall wash their hands and their feet in

water from it. When they go into the tabernacle of meeting, or when they come near the altar to minister, to burn an offering made by fire to the LORD, they shall wash with water, lest they die. So they shall wash their hands and their feet, lest they die. And it shall be a statute forever to them—to him and his descendants throughout their generations."

The two articles of furniture in the outer court, the brazen altar and the brazen laver, are both made of brass, which symbolizes sin and the judgment of sin. In the outer court the believer in Jesus is cleansed from sin by the two cleansing agents, the blood of Jesus at the brazen altar and by the Word of God at the brazen laver.

The brazen laver is in the outer court of the tabernacle, in natural light, exposed to the elements. The brazen laver is brass, made from brass mirrors of the women of Israel who served at the door of the tabernacle of meeting.[68] It was filled with water, which is the second provision in God's plan for cleansing. There is no detailed description for the brazen laver; all we know is that it is a brass container that holds water for washing.

The Brazen Laver

The Importance of the Laver

The cross is not the place to stop. But there is no further progress on the journey into the holy of holies without washing at the brazen laver. The penalty for not washing is death. God's presence is not accessible except through the outer court past the brazen altar and the brazen laver. We must be clean to come into God's presence, and He has made the provision for us to become clean. Attendance at the laver was *not optional*. It was *absolutely required* of every priest who passed from the altar to the tabernacle or from the tabernacle to the altar.

God cleanses us in the outer court and prepares us to come to Him and to fellowship with Him. At the brazen altar, the cross and the cleansing by the blood of Jesus is established in our life journey. At the brazen laver, the washing of water, the cleansing by the Word of God, is established in our life journey. At the cross God does it all for us, but then we need to begin to read the Bible and do what it says; He doesn't do this for us. This is where we need to hunger for the Word of God in our hearts. When we do what we see in the Word, it cleanses us. (See Colossians 2:11–12.) Two cleansing agents were required: blood and water. The blood cleansed the inside[69] (a new heart), and the water cleansed the outside (hands[70] and feet[71]—what comes in contact with the world.)

We have the opportunity to learn to wash ourselves in the "water of the Word."[72] The brazen laver is a type of our washing in the water of the Word. At the brazen altar everything was done *for* the worshipper; but at the brazen laver the worshipper must take initiative. Only priests were allowed past the brazen altar. Because Jesus has made us a kingdom of priests, we are all kings and priests before our God[73] and, therefore, are allowed to progress beyond the brazen altar. Once past the altar, the priest was required to wash himself. The penalty for not washing was death.[74] Coming to the brazen laver was not an optional stop. There was no continuing without washing.

When you are born again, you need to learn how to wash yourself: get where the Word is taught, read the Word, listen to the Word, and hear the Word! Wash! If we won't wash, death sets in—"lest they die." We need to participate, to cooperate by washing ourselves with the pure water of the Word. When someone will not wash in the Word after being born again, death begins to come into their spiritual life. Their growth is stunted. They fail to grow and even begin to slip back in their Christian life. Washing is the solution! We are not there yet! We need to learn to wash in the Word of God. Let's learn how to stay clean. The laver will teach us how.

The Purpose of the laver—See the Problem, Find the Solution

Remember, the laver was made from the brass mirrors of the women who served at the door of the tabernacle of meeting. These mirrors, brought from Egypt, were made of highly polished brass and were valued highly. It was a sacrifice for the serving women to give these rare treasures, yet, what a privilege! Look at the symbolism in the mirrors: when we look in a mirror, we see what we look like and see what needs changing. (Did you ever look in the mirror and not do something or want to do something about your appearance?)

The priest came to the laver, the large polished brass bowl filled with pure water, and it became a mirror when he looked in it, providing a means for him to clean himself with the water it held. Looking in the mirror revealed the problem, and the solution was available in the water. Here the priest took the responsibility to look and see if he needed to clean up. He washed his hands and his feet before progressing any farther in the tabernacle before drawing nearer to God.[75]

Let's look at the work of the altar and the laver:

The Brazen Altar	The Brazen Laver
• Deals with past sins	• Deals with present sins
• Cleanses with the blood and fire—the altar is for the rebellious heart	• Cleanses our contaminated walk with the water of the Word
• All is done *for* the priest	• It is done *by* the priest

Do you see the different purposes of the brazen altar and the brazen laver? The first function of the brazen laver is to reveal the priest to himself. He doesn't have to depend on what others think or even what he himself thinks—he can know what God thinks.

We see in John 1:1 and John 1:14 that Jesus is the Word. "In the beginning was the Word, and the Word was with God, and the Word was God...And the Word became flesh and dwelt among us." The laver is a type of Christ, the Word of God, cleansing us from the impurities of the world. The laver was used by the priests to cleanse their hands and feet. Jesus told the disciples in John 15:3, "You are clean by my word." Jesus is the Word, and the Word cleanses us when we obey it. That's what we need in order to draw near to God. We need to look in the mirror to see our state, and we need to wash in the water to get sin cleaned up. Where there is no Word, death occurs. If we don't learn to wash ourselves, death will begin to come in areas of our spiritual life.

The Three Attributes of the Laver

1 . It was a mirror

The Bible compares the Word of God to a mirror in James 1:23–24:

> "For if anyone is a hearer of the word and not a doer, he is like a man observing his natural face in a mirror; for he observes himself, goes away, and immediately forgets what kind of man he was."

2 . It was made of brass

The Bible also compares the Word of God to a judge in John 12:47–48:

> "And if anyone hears My words and does not believe, I do not judge him; for I did not come to judge the world but to save the world. He who

rejects Me, and does not receive My words has that which judges him—the word that I have spoken will judge him in that last day."

3 . It was filled with water

The Bible speaks of the Word cleansing us in Ephesians 5:25–27:

"Husbands, love your wives, just as Christ also loved the church and gave himself for her, that he might sanctify and cleanse her with the washing of water by the word."

Each of these points speaks about an attribute of the Word of God.

God's Word as a Mirror

First, the laver was a mirror. This is a type of God's Word being a mirror. Let's read James 1:23–24 again: "For if anyone is a hearer of the word and not a doer, he is like a man observing his natural face in a *mirror;* for he observes himself, goes away, and immediately forgets what kind of man he was" (emphasis added). The Word of God is a mirror. It is *not* a mirror that shows you your external physical appearance, but it shows you your inward spiritual condition.

If you want to know what you are really like in the sight of God, look in the mirror. If we will read the Bible, we will begin to see our imperfections and how to correct them. When you look in a mirror, you can do one of two things. A mirror may show you that your face needs washing, your hair needs combing, and your clothes are sloppy and dirty. You can say, "Oh, so what?" and walk away, doing nothing about what was revealed to you. In that case, the mirror does you no good at all. Or you can act on what you see and make the necessary adjustments. In this case, the mirror was useful. James 1:25 says that you will be blessed as a result of what you do.

Remember, it is not the *hearers* of the Word that are blessed; it is the *doers*. The people who act upon God's Word are the ones who are blessed. You can hear the Word preached, get all excited, shout and clap your hands, but if you don't act upon it, you will get no permanent blessing from it. The only thing you will have done is increased your responsibility before God. Matthew 7:24–27 tells us about two houses, one built on sand and the other built on the rock. The difference in the house that stood and the house that fell is that one of the builders was likened to a man who obeyed the Word. If we only hear the Word of God and fail to do what it says, our lives are not able to survive the storms of life.[76] We need to wash!

God's Word as Judge

Second, the laver was the judge. It was made of brass, which always typifies divine examination and judgment. You may ask why God's Word is our judge. Did you know God is reluctant to judge, even though He is the Righteous Judge? Jesus said in John 12:47–48,

> "And if anyone hears My words and does not believe, I do not judge him; for I did not come to judge the world but to save the world. He who rejects Me, and does not receive My words, has that which judges him—the word that I have spoken will judge him in the last day."

First Peter 1:17 tells us that God the Father is the judge. John 5:22 tells us that the Father has committed all judgment to the Son. John 5:22 says, "Moreover, the Father judges no one, but has entrusted all judgment to the Son." The Son says in John 12:47–48: I'm not going to judge you; I've committed all judgment to the Word. *God is reluctant to execute judgment, but judgment will be executed by the standard of the Word of God.*

There is an absolute standard of divine judgment, and this gives us the blessed opportunity of judging ourselves. "If we judged ourselves, we would not come under judgment." [77] Judgment by whom? God. He says: "If you will judge yourself by looking in the mirror and doing what it says, I won't have to judge you." God wants us to judge ourselves so we will not come under His judgment and He gives us His Word as the mirror.

God's Word as Cleansing Water

Third, the laver was the cleansing agent. It was filled with water, which typifies the Word of God. In Ephesians 5:25b–27 we read:

> "Christ also loved the church and gave Himself for her, that He might sanctify and cleanse her with the washing of the water by the word, that He might present her to Himself a glorious church, not having spot or wrinkle or any such thing, but that she should be holy and without blemish."

At the brazen laver, Jesus cleanses and sanctifies by the washing of the water of the Word those whom He has first redeemed by His blood at the brazen altar. Why did Christ redeem the church? Bear this in mind: Christ redeemed the church by His blood *that* He might thereafter cleanse and sanctify it with the washing of the water of the Word of God. The Father wants us with Him; sin cannot enter His presence, so He makes provision for our cleansing from sin and teaches us how to get clean! Sanctification and holiness, which fulfill God's will, depend upon the blood of the cross and upon the water of the Word.

Studying the Word of God, submitting to the Word, obeying the Word, and living by the Word gets us ready for the coming of Christ. First John 5:6 speaks of Jesus:

"This is He who came by water and blood—Jesus Christ; not only by water, but by water and blood. And it is the [Holy] Spirit who bears witness, because the Spirit is truth."

Jesus came by water as the great Teacher even before the cross. As previously stated, Jesus said to His disciples in John 15:3, "You are already clean because of the word which I have spoken to you." The Word cleanses, but He did not come by water (or word) only. Jesus is not just a great teacher. He is the Redeemer who had to shed His blood. Without the shedding of blood, there is no remission[78] of sins and no redemption. So Jesus shed His blood *that he might thereafter* cleanse and sanctify us with the washing of water of the Word. He came by water and by blood, and it is the Spirit of God that bears witness to the blood and to the Word.

When you come to the laver, you are in the area of the Spirit's witness, because the Spirit bears witness to the water (the Word) and the blood. Here in the area of strong assurance, you know without a doubt what God has done and is doing for you. *If you get away from this area, you lose the Spirit's witness.* The Spirit bears witness to the brazen altar (the blood) and the brazen laver (the Word), and that gives us the assurance to continue the journey into our next stop, which will take us to the holy place. It is in the holy place that we will understand more fully the witness of the Holy Spirit.

First Things First
One of the first things we are encouraged to do as a new Christian is to read the Bible. *We must do this for ourselves; no one can do it for us.* First, God cleanses us of the old sin nature at the time of salvation, and we bury that old man in baptism, and the sign of the new covenant is our circumcision made without hands.[79] Then we must begin to cooperate, to hunger for the milk of the Word, and start washing ourselves by giving time to the Word of God.

At the brazen laver the believer priest is able to inspect himself before drawing nearer to the presence of God. Twice God had instructed that they must wash at the laver before coming into the holy place, lest they die.[80]

The Generation That Seeks God's Face
After we have received forgiveness for sin, we as priests may proceed in our journey. We are clean inside, but we need to stay clean outside. The Word of God is the cleansing agent. It is typified in the brazen laver in the tabernacle of Moses: brass for sin, laver for water. The water of the Word reveals what needs altering, or fixing. Doing the Word, washing ourselves, cleanses

our sin outwardly and gives us clean hands. David said in Psalm 24:3–6,

> "Who may ascend the hill of the LORD? Who may stand in his holy place? He who has clean hands and a pure heart, who does not lift up his soul to an idol or swear by what is false. He will receive blessing from the LORD and vindication from God his Savior. Such is the generation of those who seek Him, who seek your face, O God of Jacob."

Jesus said in Matthew 5:8: "Blessed are the pure in heart for they shall see God."

We are that generation. We are seeking God's face. The blood from the brazen altar and the water, the pure water of the Word of God in the brazen laver, are God's cleansing agents. They are God's provision to cleanse us from defilement, to make us holy, so that we may enter in and dwell in His presence. Isn't that awesome? God wants us to be with Him. He has made all the provision—even giving the blood of the perfect sacrifice, God Himself, the spotless Lamb, to cleanse us. Then Jesus the Word of God washes us. What a mighty God we serve! Hallelujah to the Lamb who takes away the sin of the world.[81] The blood of Jesus doesn't cover sin, but "takes away, blots out" our sin!

Why does God want to redeem you? He wants you with him! That is the Father's heart. The brazen laver is part of His provision for cleansing the sin from the life of the believer so that He may dwell in God's presence.

My Story

My parents are wonderful Christians who started taking me to church when I was only one week old. When I was eight, I asked Jesus to come into my heart, and I was born again and baptized in the cold water of a creek nearby. My Sunday school teacher encouraged us to read our "daily Bible readings," and I was challenged and began to read my Bible daily. I began to wash in the Word. I knew nothing about this process or coming into the holy of holies. During those years I read the Word, but I didn't understand it. The Bible was black ink on white paper to me. I often wondered, "Is there more?" I longed to know Jesus better. I wish I would have known to ask in my childlike heart, "Are we there yet?" I was wandering around in the outer court.

I stayed in the outer court, in the natural light, for twenty years. I had heard of the secret place, but I didn't know where it was or how to get there. I really thought it was in heaven. But the Father saw my hungry heart, and He had a plan to reveal Himself to me.

In 1970, when I was twenty–eight years old, twenty years after I had been born again and began washing in the Word, God used a pregnancy that I had not planned to draw me to Himself. He created a situation that caused me to find the answer. My friend Bob Mumford says, "God will fix a fix to fix you!" And God fixed a fix for me. I became pregnant with my third child, and that was not my plan! Through that "fix" God drew me into His plan. I began seeking the Lord, and the Helper came running. The Father wanted me near Him, now. Jesus wants to take us to the Father, not just in heaven, but now, as we are living day by day; but that is for a later chapter.

Are You in the Outer Court?

A few years ago when I began learning about this pattern of the tabernacle, I read in Andrew Murray's book *The Holiest of All* that he too had stayed in the outer court for many years. He said that most Christians spend their entire lives in the outer court. In the outer court, Jesus is the terminator of sin! The blood and the water cleanse the believer from sin. Have you journeyed beyond the outer court? Don't stop here! We are not there yet! Are you enjoying the journey so far? The next chapter will take us into the holy place, past the first veil, and nearer to God's throne. We need help to finish the journey; the Helper will show us the way! God has provided the Helper to help us make the rest of the journey. We will not be able to go on without the help of the Holy Spirit.

Lord, help us cooperate with You.

We're ready to go to the next stop on our journey.

Let's continue past the veil into the holy place and find the help we are looking for. Let's press on toward our goal.[82]

CHAPTER 5

The Holy Place—Drawing Near—
Jesus the Illuminator

In this chapter we will be going from the outer court into the tabernacle itself. We will be going into the holy place. Andrew Murray has said that most Christians spend their entire lives in the outer court without coming past the veil into the holy place, and without knowing the illumination of the Holy Spirit.[83] We are on the journey into the Father's presence. God is revealing His plan to us—the provision He has made to bring us to Himself. The primary purpose of redemption is to bring God's people to Himself. His plan is so awesome, so complete, and so simple that a child can follow it. God's plan is for His people to be in His presence, and His provision is revealed in the pattern of the tabernacle of Moses.

Moving Closer to God's Presence

This next leg of our journey is a major step. We will go from the outer court into the tabernacle itself, which is the building located in the outer court. We will come closer to God's presence, into the covered tabernacle, past the first veil, into the holy place. In this chapter we enter the second division: the holy place.

There is a lot of difference between the outer court and the holy place. There is a veil that covers the entrance into the holy place, and this veil is not sheer; you cannot see inside without going inside. (Much like the seven–and–a–half–foot–high curtain that surrounded the outer court cannot be seen over but can be entered through the gate.) The light is different in the holy place; without the illumination of the Holy Spirit, we are in the dark. Are you afraid to let Holy Spirit lead you? Many are afraid to move out of the outer court, and there are many reasons why Christians stay in the outer court and never enter into the holy place. One of the great hindrances is the tradition of men. Many Christians are afraid of the Holy Spirit. When we get born again and begin to wash ourselves with the Word of God, we think we have arrived and fail to seek more of Jesus. Many times this is all we have been taught and for one reason or another we failed to seek the Lord, and we read His word with our denominational glasses on.

God wants us to know. If we will but ask Him, He will reveal the path to us. Fear also keeps many Christians from the pursuit of God. They are so afraid of being deceived that they don't go on. They fear man more than they fear the Lord. Some fear persecution, being called a fanatic or "Jesus Freak," and there is persecution that comes in pursuing God.

Counting the Cost

Everything that is worth anything costs something. It takes time and boldness to seek the Lord; most of the time the Spirit of the Lord does not just "come upon us." Some of us are just too lazy. God loves a seeker; He is a seeker, and He wants us to seek Him. He always rewards the seeker. Hebrews 11:6 says, "In order to please God we must believe that He is and that He is a rewarder of those who diligently seek Him." So let's seek diligently to enter into the Holy of Holies. Diligent means: To seek after carefully, quietly and steadily persevering especially in detail or exactness. Don't quit! The reason that we have the blood and the water in the outer court is to prepare us to come into the holy place so that we will be ready for the Holy of Holies. We are not there yet. These cleansing agents deal with the sin that separate us from Father God. The blood and the water do bear witness to the Holy Spirit.

You have what you need to enter in if you have the blood of Jesus and if you are reading the word of God and doing what it says. It is the Holy Spirit who will show the way into the Holiest. If you are having any trouble making this transition, ask Holy Spirit to come and help you. It is the Father's good pleasure to bring you into His presence. So come on; let's go on. Let's set our hearts to pursue and press in and pay the price to continue. Pray this simple prayer: *Holy Spirit, come and help me. I need the Helper to show me the way into the Holy of Holies.*

The Transition

The holy place is a place of transition. We leave behind the natural light of the outer court, which represents what we perceive with our senses, and enter the area that is illuminated only by the light of the golden lamp stand, which typifies our being dependent on the Holy Spirit to reveal spiritual truths to us. We also leave behind the brass articles in the outer court—the brass symbolizing sin and judgment—and find that all the furniture in the holy place and the holy of holies is made of gold, which symbolizes purity and deity. We leave behind the natural for the supernatural.

We are making progress—but we are not there yet. Our destination is God's throne, the mercy seat, in the Holy of Holies. As we draw near—our Helper, the Holy Spirit, is available to lead and guide and to bring us into all truth, for He is the Spirit of truth.

At the brazen altar, God did it all for us. Even though we have had our sins forgiven and have found peace with God through Jesus, *we are not there yet.* So far in our journey we have made two stops; we visited two articles of furniture in the outer court. At the brazen altar, the blood of Jesus redeems us, and we come out of darkness into His marvelous light.[84] His blood has justified us—it is just as though we had never sinned—and His blood is cleansing us: "But if we walk in the light as He is in the light, we have fellowship with one another, and the blood of Jesus Christ His Son cleanses us from all sin" (1 John 1:7).

We moved from the brazen altar, symbolic of the cross of Jesus, to the brazen laver that is filled with pure water and is symbolic of the Word of God. The brazen altar, the cross, prepares us to go on to the brazen laver, the Word that washes; but it is the Word that effects the necessary changes in us to continue the journey. To go beyond the outer court, we must go to the laver, the cleansing and sanctifying Word. We must wash with the water of the Word of God; we must look in the mirror and wash off the sin that is revealed. In the old covenant the priest was required to wash before he went into the tabernacle. As priests, we too must wash in the Word, the laver. The brazen altar and the brazen laver prepare us for the holy place, where we ask for and receive help from the Holy Spirit, who is God's provision for us.

In this chapter we are overviewing the Holy Place. Let's look once again at a sketch of the tabernacle of Moses.

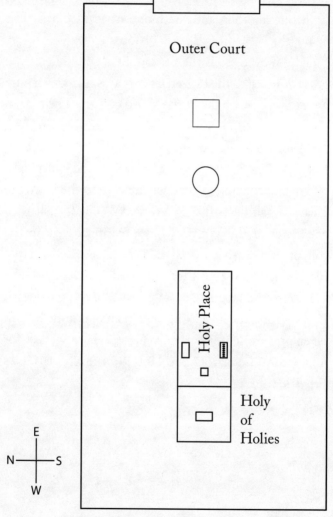

Diagram of the Tabernacle of Moses

We have seen that there are three areas of the tabernacle, making it a triune structure:

- The outer court
- The holy place
- The Holy of Holies

The obvious distinction in the tabernacle is the *type of light* available in each area.

- The outer court has natural light, which typifies the senses or knowledge gained through the five senses. When we depend on our own understanding, the Word of God is only black ink on white paper. There is no inspiration or illumination apart from the Holy Spirit.

- The holy place was illuminated by the seven-branched golden lampstand, which typifies revealed truth. When the Holy Spirit helps us, the Word of God comes alive—illuminated. It is no longer black ink on white paper. The light bulb in our mind goes on, and we get the "Ah ha!" "Oh, yes!" and, "I see!"

- The Holy of Holies had no light but that of the supernatural presence of almighty God. We learned this is the Shekinah glory of God, or His abiding presence.

In the outer court, we are cleansed from sin. We are approaching the holy place where we will receive the illumination of the Holy Spirit to be filled with and guided by Him into the Holy of Holies. In the presence of the Lord, in the Shekinah glory, is where I want to be. In the secret place of the Most High—under His shadow, under His wings is where I want to dwell! Because you are pursuing this study I know that this is also your desire; your heart gives you away, as Don Nori says in *The Secrets of the Most Holy*.

The Tabernacle

The tabernacle was the portable dwelling place for the presence of God. Wherever the Israelites moved, the tabernacle went with them. They set it up in the center of their camp. *The tabernacle sat in the outer court*, surrounded by the linen fence. It had four layers of covering and was not attractive outwardly. The beauty was within: God's glory is seen by the worshipper who comes into His presence, not by the spectator who looks on from a distance. Remember, God works from the inside out (He looks at the heart); if we want to find out what is inside, we must take the step of faith and enter. Under the Old Covenant the tabernacle was the place of God's dwelling. In the New Covenant it is the pattern into God's presence, His dwelling place.

Overview of the Holy Place

There were two compartments or divisions in the forty–five–feet–long by fifteen–feet–wide tabernacle that is in the outer court. The holy place, the first division, was thirty feet long and fifteen feet wide; and the Holy of Holies, the second division, was fifteen feet square. A heavy veil separated the two areas.[85] This is the veil that was torn from top to bottom at the moment Jesus gave up His life.[86] There was another veil at the entrance of the tabernacle, called the first veil. The tabernacle can be seen outside the linen curtain fence that surrounds the outer court because it is fifteen feet high, and the curtain is seven and a half feet high.

In the first division of the covered tabernacle, the holy place, there are three articles of furniture—the golden lampstand, the golden table of showbread, and the golden altar. When we pass the first veil, it is the light from the golden lampstand that illuminates all three articles of furniture. The furniture in the holy place is made of gold. (All the furniture in the covered tabernacle is gold, contrasted to the brass in the outer court.)

- The seven–branched golden lampstand (Exodus 25:31–40) is the only source of light in the holy place.

- The golden table of showbread. Its purpose was to hold the showbread that gave life to the priests and provided a place for fellowship/communion.

- The golden altar of incense (Exodus 30:1–10), located immediately in front of the entrance to the Holy of Holies, was used for offering incense. It is the place the priests worship and intercede.

The light from the golden lampstand illuminates the holy place. This is a type of the Holy Spirit illuminating our minds. When our minds are illuminated by the Holy Spirit, we are able to understand the Word of God. When our minds make the decision to obey the Word of God, the Word of God changes us, and our minds are renewed and illuminated by the Holy Spirit. The light from the golden lampstand reveals the lampstand itself, the golden table of showbread, and the golden altar.

The Way
There is a way, a pattern that reveals the way from the brazen altar step by step—progressively—into the place where God reveals himself in his glory personally. Derek Prince has said (and I have found this to be true in my relationship with the Lord),

> There is a way into the holiest. Under the old covenant God gave a pattern to Moses. It was an earthly pattern of heavenly realities and truths. It

is now through the new covenant in Jesus Christ that we can enter by faith into the heavenly realities that were shown to Moses as a shadow, type, or pattern under the old covenant. Under the old Mosaic Covenant, the way into the holiest was not yet open.[87]

Hebrews 9:8 states, "The Holy Spirit indicating this, that the way into the holiest of all was not yet made manifest while the first tabernacle was still standing." The way was not plain or evident. But Hebrews 10:19 speaks of the new covenant, "Therefore, brethren, having boldness to enter the holiest by the blood of Jesus," that Jesus is the way into the Holy of Holies. *But most Christians never enter.* We begin the journey but stay in the outer court, never coming into God's presence, where we are created to dwell.

When the Bible speaks of "the way," I believe and have found in my daily walk that there *is* "the way" into God's presence (Hebrews 9:8). When I follow that way, I always by faith come into his presence—and I love it! By following the pattern, you too can always by faith come into God's presence. It's not a matter of guesswork or hoping; it's a matter of going by the directions of the Scripture. It is by faith. God's Word says I can come into God's presence by the blood of Jesus; therefore, I can!

The Holy Place

At this stage of the journey into God's presence, God is calling us out of the natural into the supernatural. He is calling us apart, to be a holy people. God said, "Come out from among them and be separate…Do not touch what is unclean, and I will receive you. I will be a Father to you, and you shall be my sons and daughters" (2 Corinthians 6:17–18). We could say, "Come out of the outer court and enter the holy place!"

The holy place and the Holy of Holies are smaller areas than the outer court. God is calling us to a narrower place. This next stop in our journey is a step of faith because you can't see inside until you get inside. The farther we go, the more confined the area becomes, and the options become fewer. In the end, when we come into the holiest, we will be in the smallest, most confined area of the tabernacle: a fifteen–foot square with only the ark and the mercy seat—nothing but God.

God wants you to want Him without wanting anything else at all. It's not God plus…

- Blessing
- Healing
- Revelation

It's just God. *That's what the tabernacle speaks about—those that want to meet with God, not for the sake of getting something, but because He is God.* There is no higher privilege than just getting to meet with God. The tabernacle is the pattern; it shows us the way into the holiest. This is the priestly privilege: drawing near to God and worshipping Him. God has made us a kingdom of priests, a holy people, set apart for Him.

God is calling us to be holy. Second Corinthians 7:1 says: "Therefore having these promises, beloved, let us cleanse ourselves from all filthiness of the flesh and spirit, perfecting holiness in the fear of God." His call is to come out, to be separate, and to come in to the holy place. God is calling us to open our hearts and to draw near. He is calling us to keep ourselves pure.

If we can get one thing here, we will make great progress in achieving our objective of finding the secret place. That objective is to create the longing to get into God's presence, the holiest of all, the secret place, and to be headed in one direction only: to come through the first veil, not to keep walking, wandering around in the outer court. In your heart is the hunger; you know there is more.

Holiness

We have been made holy—not by our own work—but by the finished work of Jesus. We have been able to progress toward our Holy God because we have been made holy. Andrew Murray said, "The very word 'Holy' gives us a clue to the nature of the holy place."[88]

Word Study: *holy* Hebrew *haagios* (*hag*–ee–oss); Strong's #40[89]: Compare *Hagiographa* and *hagiography*. Sacred, pure, blameless, consecrated, separated, properly revered, worthy of veneration, Godlikeness, God's innermost nature, set apart for God, reserved for God and his service. Since nothing that is polluted could be *hagios*, purity becomes a big part of *hagios*. A holy God calls for a holy people.[90]

At this point, going from natural light into illuminated light, many get bogged down. This is where we must press and pursue and seek God. Paul said in Philippians 3:13–14: "I do not count myself to have apprehended; but one thing I do, forgetting those things which are behind and reaching forward to those things which are ahead, I press toward the goal for the prize of the upward call of God in Christ Jesus." As the way gets narrower, we must press, pursue. That's why we need help. God gives us the Holy Spirit, the Helper, to show us the way, to lead and guide us into all truth.

Hunger for God is a blessing with a promise: "Blessed are those who hunger and thirst for righteousness, for they shall be filled" (Matthew 5:6). To have a heart that longs for the presence of God, we will need to practice coming to the light. Practice! John 3:21 tells us: "But he who practices the truth comes to the light, so that his deeds may be manifested as having been wrought in God."[91] The illumination of the golden lampstand will show us the way into the Holy of Holies. We need discipline and perseverance. If we don't quit, we will win!

Rewards for the Seeker

We are not on a wild goose chase. The Father is a rewarder of them that diligently seek Him (Hebrews 11:6)! He gives the Holy Spirit to them that ask. See what Jesus said in Luke 11:9: "If you then, being evil, know how to give good gifts to your children, how much more will your heavenly Father give the Holy Spirit to those who ask him!" Those who seek, find.

The Holy Spirit is here to help us make the transition from the outer court to the holy place, where we will go from natural light to the illumination of the Holy Spirit Himself. We will be going one step closer to the presence of God! So as the blood and the water, the outer court, bear witness with the Holy Spirit,[92] our Helper, the Holy Spirit, is at hand to assist us in our journey. Jesus promised that He would send us a Helper.[93] Jesus said that He (the Spirit of truth, the Holy Spirit) would lead and guide us into all truth.

We are entering the holy place through the first veil, the linen curtain, through Jesus our righteousness. Everything that we need to complete our journey into the Father's presence is available to us in Jesus. Andrew Murray has said, "Under the old covenant only the priests could come past the brazen altar—only priests could enter the holy place—but Jesus has made the way into the holiest open to the feeblest believer *(the kingdom of priests)* through His blood by faith."[94] Once we have accepted His sacrifice on the cross, once we are born again, His Spirit comes to live within us. The Holy Spirit dwelling in us gives us the help we need. *We need your help, Holy Spirit. Come and show us the way into the Holy of Holies.*

Entering the Holy Place

We are entering the holy place. A second veil separated the holy place from the Holy of Holies in the old covenant, but now that veil is gone; the veil between the holy place and the holy of Holies was torn from top to bottom when Jesus died for us. Now there is nothing that separates us from the presence of God if we will draw near. Can you sense God drawing you? As we draw near to God, He draws near to us[95]—it's a two–way proposition!

Holy Spirit is here to help us, to fill us. This is a major move. We are changing light, from the natural to the illumination of the Holy Spirit. We come through a veil, which takes us from seeing with natural light (our understanding) into seeing with the illumination of the Holy Spirit (walking in faith in the supernatural). We are trusting in the ability of the Holy Spirit and leaving behind our own abilities. Because of the veil, we can't see inside until we get inside. We need the help of the Holy Spirit. Andrew Murray has said, "It is the Spirit dwelling in us that will fit us for dwelling in God's presence."[96]

The holy place is the place of fellowship. In the holy place, we fellowship with the Holy Spirit and get acquainted with Him. We also fellowship with the other priests and with Jesus, our Great High Priest! It is a place to eat the bread of his presence and a place to give worship and intercession to God. Our fellowship is feasting on the Word, with the Holy Spirit revealing and enabling us to receive. Our full hearts overflow with worship and intercession at the golden altar as we minister to the Lord.

Are we there yet? No, our destination is the Holy of Holies, God's dwelling place. We are entering the holy place, the place nearest to God's presence, but God did not dwell there. The light from the Lampstand will reveal the way into the Holy of Holies. In the next three chapters we will spend time at each article of furniture in the holy place. Each piece will progressively prepare us for our destination—the Holy of Holies.

Come Boldly

Let's come past the first veil and step into our new surroundings. We have made the decision. We have gone from the natural light in the outer court to the supernatural illumination of the Holy Spirit in the holy place. We have seen the furniture of brass in the outer court, which typified sin and judgment be changed to the furniture made of pure gold in the holy place, which typify the deity and glory of Christ. We have experienced the wonder of God's provision at the brazen altar when the precious blood of Jesus blotted out our sin. At the brazen altar we were not in need of help because all was done for us. But there came a time, at the brazen laver, when we saw our need to wash ourselves in the pure water of the Word of God. We realized, as we looked into the mirror of the Word, that we are in need of help. We didn't want to spend our entire lives in the outer court, and we responded to the invitation to come farther. It is in the holy place that He invites us to draw near to the throne of grace to find mercy and grace.[97]

> Let's pray: *Father, we come boldly before the throne of grace to receive God's mercy and to find grace to help in the time of need. Thank you for the gift of the Holy Spirit. Welcome, Holy Spirit, lead us and guide us into all truth. Thank you, Holy Spirit, that you are helping us finish our journey into God's presence, in Jesus's name, amen.*

CHAPTER 6

The Golden Lampstand—
Receiving Illumination

The Tabernacle of Moses is a pattern—a map. You know you don't have to have a map to get somewhere; you don't have to have a pattern to make a piece of furniture, a dress, or a gingerbread house. But if you don't know "how to," a pattern or map is invaluable. I live about eighty miles from Nashville, Tennessee. I was a child the first time I went to Nashville; Mother and Daddy took me. I rode with them then, but now I know how to go there myself. They gave me the map and now I go where I desire in Nashville. A teacher is of great value. The lack of a good teacher is one reason many do not find the way into the Holy of Holies.

We have the map, or directions (pattern), and the teacher to guide us to our destination. For the journey to Nashville, the pattern was the driving directions, and the teachers were Mother and Daddy. In our journey into the presence of God, our pattern is the tabernacle, and our teacher is the Holy Spirit. Many believers abide in God's presence without knowledge of the tabernacle's pattern. However, the pattern gives a simple step–by–step guide for our journey into the Holy of Holies.

This chapter takes us to the first article of furniture in the holy place: the golden lampstand. Light from the golden lampstand filled the holy place with a soft light shimmering off the golden walls, giving light for the priests to fellowship with one another and minister to the Lord. Don't we all look better in candlelight? My flaws are much easier to take in soft shimmering light! The remainder of our journey into the Holy of Holies will be without natural light. It is at the lampstand that we receive light to continue our journey.

As our eyes adjust from the natural light in the outer court to the light from the lampstand, we can see the three pieces of furniture in the holy place—the golden lampstand that gives light; the golden table of showbread, where the priests eat and fellowship; and we see the golden altar, where we can worship the Lord and intercede.

The Seven–branched Golden Lampstand

Exodus 40:24–25 reads, "He [Moses] put the lampstand in the tabernacle of meeting, across from the table, on the south side of the tabernacle; and he lit the lamps before the LORD, as the LORD had commanded

Moses." The golden lampstand is the only illumination in the holy place.

The lampstand[98] was hammered out of one piece of solid gold, weighing between seventy–five and one hundred and twenty–five pounds! It was not poured or molded but beaten. It had seven branches—a large central shaft with six branches that formed three perfect pairs on either side.

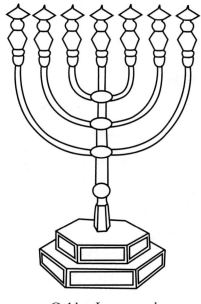

Golden Lampstand

Seven is the number of perfection, and Jesus is the perfect manifestation of God. The number of branches is a type of the seven characteristics of the Holy Spirit.

Revelation 4:5 shows us, "And from the throne proceeded lightnings, thunderings, and voices. Seven lamps of fire were burning before the throne, which are the seven Spirits of God." The solid gold lampstand is symbolic of Jesus, the light of the world. The oil and fire are types of the Holy Spirit. God's Spirit is manifested in heaven as "seven lamps of fire burning before the throne." Isaiah 11:2 gives us the names of these characteristics or manifestations of the Holy Spirit, "And the...

- Spirit of the Lord shall rest upon Him (the central shaft)
- The Spirit of wisdom and understanding
- The Spirit of counsel and might
- The Spirit of knowledge and the fear of the LORD."

The Spirit of the Lord is the central shaft, and the three pairs of branches complete the lampstand. The oil of the Holy Spirit fills all seven of the branches on the lampstand. He gives light to all. The lampstand is in the midst of the seven churches as described in Revelation 1:20, 4:5. It shed its light before the Lord and leads us to God's purpose. Thus, the Holy Spirit leads us to God.

The golden lampstand provides light for the holy place. The Holy Spirit is God's provision for us— supernatural illumination. We are not led by natural light. (Romans 8: 14: "For as many as are led by the Spirit of God, these are sons of God.") As priests we don't have to eat in darkness; we have illumination in the holy place. I like to think of myself asking for help and having the Holy Spirit lead me into the holy place. Can you just imagine the light from the lampstand illuminating all the gold in the holy place? The light shone on the golden walls, the three articles of furniture made from pure gold, and the priests fellowshipping in the soft glow of the lampstand's light and eating the showbread—the bread that had been exposed to the presence of the Lord for seven days. Yum, yum! This is the place where the Holy Spirit reveals Jesus to us. Let's visit the lampstand and obey the command in Ephesians 5:18 to be filled with the Holy Spirit.

The Lampstand's Purpose

1. *The lampstand reveals the lampstand*

   The first purpose of the lampstand was to reveal itself. The seven lamps of the lampstand reveal the lampstand. Exodus 25:37 reads: "You shall make seven lamps for it, and they shall arrange its lamps so that they give light in front of it." The light from the lampstand reveals the lampstand itself, just as the Holy Spirit reveals Jesus to the believer. It is a type and shadow of how the Holy Spirit reveals Jesus to the saints, the worshippers. He glorifies Jesus.[99]

2 . *The lampstand illuminates the golden table of showbread*

The second purpose of the lampstand was to illuminate the golden table of showbread, as we see in Exodus 40:24. "He put the lamp stand in the tabernacle of meeting, across from the table." The lampstand reveals the showbread on the table. The showbread is a type of Christ. Jesus tells His disciples in John 6:57, "As the living Father sent Me, and I live because of the Father, so He who feeds on Me will live because of Me." Judson Cornwall said, "Fellowship that is intimate requires a very special light—the light of the Holy Spirit. It could never be done in darkness. Nothing God does is in the dark."[100] It is Satan who works in darkness. God gives light. Satan wants a dark and confused mind; God wants our minds to be illuminated by the Holy Spirit. The lampstand illuminates the table and reveals the bread of His presence, the showbread that the priest will feast upon!

3 . *The lampstand illuminates the golden altar*

The third purpose of the lampstand is to illuminate the golden altar. At the golden altar the priests are able to give worship to God and to intercede in the light of the lampstand. Without the lampstand the priest would have to worship and pray in darkness. The Holy Spirit makes us effective in prayer and worship.[101] The Holy

Spirit prays through us the will of God. Romans 8:26–27 states, "Likewise the Spirit also helps in our weaknesses. For we do not know what we should pray for as we ought, but the Spirit Himself makes intercession for us with groanings, which cannot be uttered. Now He who searches the hearts knows what the mind of the Spirit is, because He makes intercession for the saints according to the will of God." The Holy Spirit glorifies Jesus.

The Lampstand revealed and illuminated:

- The lampstand
- The table of showbread
- The golden altar

The light of the Lampstand reveals Jesus, who is the Lampstand. He immerses us in the Holy Spirit who gives us light to finish the journey.

The lampstand reveals what God has for us. Everything in the holy place was done in the light of the golden lampstand. It was placed on the south wall of the holy place near the first veil. The lampstand illuminated all of the activities in the holy place. The light from the lampstand reveals the table of showbread that holds the bread that gives us life.[102] There is a table prepared for us—we have the help of the Holy Spirit and other priests in a holy atmosphere. The bread fills us and causes us to grow and mature. So we have the Holy Spirit revealing the table of showbread: the lampstand manifested the availability of the bread of His presence. Eating the bread was required to continue the journey. As we go from the table to the altar we can see into the Holy of Holies. The lampstand illuminates the opening where the veil was removed, torn from top to bottom, through the death of Jesus.

The light from lampstand reveals the golden altar. The Holy Spirit helps us worship and intercede at the golden altar. The golden altar is the place where we can overflow with worship and intercession. Our intercession and worship is like incense,[103] a sweet fragrance before God.

Symbolism of the Lampstand

The lampstand is a type of Christ:

- Jesus is the Messiah, who shall redeem His people and reveal God. (See Matthew 1:21, Luke 2:32.)

- Jesus is the light of the world. (See John 8:12, 1 John 1:5, Revelation 21:23–24)

The lampstand was made of beaten gold, solid gold— symbolic of purity and royalty.

- Jesus was shaped (beaten like the gold) in the following ways
  - He came to earth

- Was born in a manger
- Had a very young (teenage) mother
- Had a small beginning—his ministry began not in a great temple or before a large crowd but at a small wedding
- He was rejected by His own brothers and sisters
- Scoffed at by His own countrymen
- Mocked in His home town

The hammering didn't stop there. The elders rose up against Him, so he had to leave town to avoid being thrown over a cliff. Do you see the beaten gold—the hammering that formed Him? Being formed is a hammering process as we see in 1 Peter 4:12: "Beloved, do not think it strange concerning the fiery trial which is to try you, as though some strange thing happened to you;" our lives are hammered out just as Jesus's was.

We see Jesus, the dying Lamb, become the risen Lord. Judson Cornwall said, "Jesus is the very God of the very God. He is heaven's glory (pure gold), resplendent with life, opulent with beauty and abundantly fruitful!"[104]

The oil and the fire are types of the Holy Spirit:

- Oil being a type of the Holy Spirit is inferred in many scriptural references: Exodus 27:20, 1 Samuel 16:13, and others. The oil produced light in the holy place.

- The Holy Spirit and fire are spoken of in Matthew 3:11 and Acts 2:3–4, and the typology is inferred throughout the Scriptures.

The oil is a type of the Holy Spirit; He will light our way and give us entrance into the Holy of Holies. Hebrews 9:8a states: "the Holy Spirit indicating this, that the way into the Holiest of all was not yet made manifest" or open, in the old covenant. But in chapter ten verse nineteen and twenty–two we read, "Therefore, brethren, having boldness to enter the Holiest by the blood of Jesus" (v 19). "Let us draw near with a true heart in full assurance of faith, having our hearts sprinkled from an evil conscience and our bodies washed with pure water" (v 22). After Jesus shed His blood, we received the commandment to "come boldly" and enter in. The Holy Spirit leads the way. This is the new and living way, the new covenant in Jesus.

What Jesus Said about the Holy Spirit

Just before Jesus was crucified, he told us in John chapters fourteen, fifteen, and sixteen that He was going to send us help. He would not leave us alone. He said, "I will not leave you alone, I will give you another Helper just like me—it will be better for you if I go away" (because when He was seated at the right hand of the Father He would send the Holy Spirit—Acts 1:4, 2:33). In John 14:15–18 Jesus said,

> If you love Me, keep My commandments. And I will pray the Father, and He will give you another Helper, that He may abide with you forever—the Spirit of truth, whom the world cannot receive, because it neither sees Him nor knows Him; but you know Him, for He dwells with you and will be in you. I will not leave you orphans; I will come to you.

He also said in John 16:7b, "It is to your advantage that I go away; for if I do not go away, the Helper will not come to you; but if I depart, I will send Him to you."

After Jesus died, rose from the dead, and ascended to the Father, He sent the Promise of the Father. We have a Helper on our journey. We can't complete our journey without stopping at the golden lampstand and getting filled up! The Holy Spirit will lead us and guide us into the presence of God.

Here is what Jesus says about the Holy Spirit in John chapters fourteen, fifteen, and sixteen:

- John 14:26—He will teach you all things

- John 14:26—He will bring to your remembrance all things that Jesus said to you

- John 15:26—He will testify of Me (Jesus)

- John 16:8–11—He will convict the world of sin, righteousness, and judgment
- John 16:13—He will guide you into all truth
- John 16:13—He will not speak on his own authority, but whatever he hears he will speak
- John 16:13—He will tell you things to come
- John 16:14—He will glorify Him (Jesus)
- John 16:14—He will take of what is mine (Jesus) and declare it to you

Notice that Jesus always calls the Holy Spirit "He," not "it." Holy Spirit is a person; He is the third person of the Godhead. Jesus sent the Holy Spirit to help us. He said He would send another like Himself:

Word Study: *another, allos, (al*–loss); Strong's # 243:[105] One besides, another of the same kind. The word shows similarities but diversities of operation and ministries. Jesus' use of *allos* for sending another Comforter equals "one besides Me and in addition to Me but one just like Me. He will do in My absence what I would do if I were physically present with you." The Spirit's coming assures continuity with what Jesus did and taught.[106]

Jesus is the Baptizer in the Holy Spirit. John the Baptist announced Jesus as the Baptizer in the Holy Spirit in Matthew 3:11, Mark 1:8, Luke 3:16, and

John 1:33 and some of Jesus's last words were, "For John truly baptized with water, but you shall be baptized with the Holy Spirit not many days from now" (Acts 1:5). Paul repeats Jesus's words in Acts 11:16.

> Word Study: *Baptize*, Greek *baptizo*, "to cause something to be dipped into a fluid and taken out again."[107]

Jesus baptizes us, immerses us in the Holy Spirit, giving us the help we need to live this life and to bring us to the Father. Jesus gave the pattern in John 7:37. In Acts 2:38, Peter says, "Repent, be baptized and you shall receive the gift of the Holy Spirit." Do you see how the Holy Spirit's light surrounds or immerses the believer in Himself, in the holy place? Have you let Jesus baptize you in the Holy Spirit?

Jesus is not jealous of the Holy Spirit—Father, Son, Holy Spirit are all One God. There is unity in the Trinity. The Holy Spirit glorifies Jesus; the Holy Spirit is the promise of the Father.

The Holy Place—a Place of Ministry
Our journey has brought us to the holy place, to the golden lampstand filled with pure oil. The Holy Spirit reveals Jesus here, in the holy place as the Light of the World, as the Bread of Life, and as our Great Intercessor. Have you let the Holy Spirit fill you? In John 7:37b–39a Jesus said, "If anyone thirsts, let him

come to Me and drink. He who believes in me, as the Scripture has said, out of his heart will flow rivers of living water." "But this he spoke concerning the Spirit…" Do you see the *pattern* here to receive the Holy Spirit?

- Thirst
- Come
- Drink
- Out of your hearts flow

Peter also gave instruction in the verse just quoted, Acts 2:38: repent, be baptized—receive the gift of the Holy Spirit.

When an individual is born again, the Holy Spirit baptizes him into the body of Christ.[108] He is baptized in water by man.[109] And Jesus is the one who baptizes in the Holy Spirit.[110] *Jesus, thank You for sending the promise of the Father. I want You, Jesus, to immerse me in the Holy Spirit.*

My Story
When I was eight years old, I received Jesus's free gift of salvation; I was born again, I was baptized in water, and began to read my Bible daily. I didn't know there was more to the journey at that time. I didn't know about the power of the Holy Spirit to illuminate my life and give me power to love and serve Jesus. And

although I did long to know Jesus more, I wandered around in the outer court for twenty years! (Look back at the diagram of the tabernacle. It is a straight shot from the gate to the mercy seat. But I took a few detours—I didn't know the way!)

Before I became pregnant with our third child (the fix that fixed me in chapter four), I had my life pretty well planned out. We had our three–bedroom house that was just right for our two girls and us. It was not my idea to be pregnant! When our baby was born, he had to be whisked away to Vanderbilt Hospital in Nashville. He had inhaled the amniotic fluid, which caused him to have aspiration pneumonia; he hung between life and death for several days. I remember well that morning after he was born—the emptiness that I felt being in the maternity ward without a baby! A few months earlier I had read Catherine Marshall's book *Beyond Ourselves,* and she told of Peter Marshall's sermon and the example he gave of the broken toy:

> Suppose a child has a broken toy. He brings the toy to his father, saying that he himself has tried to fix it and has failed. He asks his father to do it for him. The father gladly agrees, takes the toy, and begins to work. Now obviously the father can do his work most quickly and easily if the child makes no attempt to interfere, simply sits quietly watching, or even goes about other business, with never a doubt that the toy is being successfully mended. But what do most of God's children do

in such a situation? Often we stand by offering a lot of meaningless advice and some rather silly criticism. We even get impatient and try to help, and so get in the Father's way, generally hindering the work... Finally, in our desperation, we may even grab the toy out of the Father's hands entirely, saying rather bitterly that we hadn't really thought he could fix it anyway... that we'd given him a chance and he had failed us. [111]

This is what I did with our sick baby. I would give our sick baby, my burden, to God but soon take it back again. I knew God could heal, but I didn't know "healing" was who He is—Jehovah Rapha, the God that healeth thee—Exodus 15:26. Because I hadn't been released by my doctor to go to Vanderbilt, my mother and I stayed at home and prayed, while my daddy and my husband were in Nashville with baby Paul. God, though, was teaching me this: He is my Father, full of mercy, and He was using this hard time to teach me to trust. In late March 1971 when Paul was six days old, we brought him home to his two sisters, Jenny Lynne (almost eight years old) and Susannah (four years old). The doctor told us, "It is the same as though he had never been sick!" Paul and I were overjoyed. (This baby is now our pastor at Church on the Hill in Algood, Tennessee!)

I so wanted to pay God back for answering my prayer, and I guess I thought I could. But I already did all I knew to do—I read my Bible and prayed every day, we went to church, we gave our tithe, I was faithful to my husband, and we didn't drink, smoke, or chew! But hunger to know God more was growing inside of me (I was getting thirsty), and I began to seek God the first thing in the morning after I got the girls off to school. I remember praying, "Lord, make me 'on fire' like the apostles in Acts. What made the disciples in the book of Acts so fiery?" I went visiting every Thursday morning at our church to invite people to church—but as I look back now, I didn't tell them about my relationship with Jesus; I just invited them to church! I had been born again, but I didn't have the power of God working in my life to witness for Jesus. Jesus said, "You shall receive power when the Holy Spirit comes upon you to be my witnesses." I was ignorant of the Holy Spirit's power. But Father God, full of mercy, was teaching me—and was I ever getting thirsty.

I didn't know about being filled with the Holy Spirit, but one morning as I read in Billy Graham's *Decision Magazine* a section called "The Quiet Heart," I read the verse in John 14:20: "In that day you will know that I am in My Father, and you in Me, and I in you." I had read this verse many times because I had read the book of John through many times. But that morning that verse came alive to me! I remembered three or four times when God tried to get my attention to satisfy my thirst for Him. But by my actions I said, "Not now, let me run the show—don't leave me, Jesus, but I will figure this out!" I didn't know I was not yielding to Jesus.

As I pondered this verse in John, I saw a picture of my heart, and it was black as coal soot! I felt like I could just reach in and pull out the filth! I knew it was sin in my heart. And I knew what my sin was: jealousy, bitterness, and envy and especially self–righteousness!—sins of the heart. I didn't know that sin was there. But as I began to seek God, he showed me my need to be cleaned up. But then, in the very bottom of my heart I saw light that was about the size of the head of a straight pin, and it was that indescribable light that I knew was Jesus. I had pushed Jesus all the way to the bottom, but He had kept His Word "never to leave me or forsake me." I said, "Jesus, fill my whole heart with that light!" And He did—whoosh! I didn't even know what had happened to me! But the joy, joy, joy, joy—down in my heart—that I had sung about all my life overflowed in my heart, and the Bible that had been like reading black ink on the white paper came alive to me. I couldn't wait to read the Bible. I didn't have to; I got to! It was like reading the morning newspaper—it was current and alive! The Holy Spirit had filled my heart. Now all these years later the Holy Spirit is more wonderful than ever because He makes Jesus so real to me!

Before then I didn't know that I needed to be filled with the Holy Spirit or that I could be; but when I cried out, God did fill my heart with His light. At that time I knew nothing about the pattern of the tabernacle I am teaching today. But Proverbs 4:5 says, "Get wisdom! Get understanding!" and Proverbs 4:7 says, "Wisdom is the principal thing; therefore get wisdom. And in all your getting, get understanding." This pattern that we are learning from the tabernacle gives understanding in how to find the secret place and come into the presence of God.

When the Holy Spirit became my Helper, He began to teach me. The Holy Spirit knows the heart of the Father (1 Corinthians 2). He helps me worship. He helps me pray. I am unable to worship or intercede effectively without the help of the Holy Spirit. He turns the light on and illuminates me. He knows what the Father desires. He is able to help me intercede according to the will of the Father. Matthew 6:10 quotes Jesus: "Your kingdom come. Your will be done on earth as it is in heaven." The Holy Spirit is able to put the desire of the Father in my heart. When I cooperate with the Holy Spirit, I can speak the will of Father into the things of earth. We can cooperate with God and "call those things which do not exist as though they do."[112] "For we walk by faith, not by sight" (2 Corinthians 5:7). The Holy Spirit enables the believer to speak and declare the will of God into existence here on earth! How awesome!

Where are you? You don't have to wander around in the outer court after you have been cleansed by the blood of Jesus. Do you find yourself in that place today of wanting more of God? Are you hungry and thirsty for more of Jesus? Have you received the Holy Spirit since you believed? That's the question Paul asked the believers at Ephesus in Acts 19! When you have repented and have been baptized, you shall receive the gift of the Holy Spirit. Jesus did not leave you alone! We have a Helper who is just like Jesus! Hallelujah! Welcome him. Receive his power to finish the journey.

Light to Finish the Journey

It is here in the holy place that the Holy Spirit gives us the light to finish our journey. We must have His help to complete our journey. We cannot make this journey on our own. In the outer court—at the cross—we are cleansed from sin and washed by the Word of God. In the outer court our cleansing makes us ready for heaven. We, this clean temple,[113] enter the holy place. There we receive supernatural help, being filled with the power of the Holy Spirit. In the holy place we are filled with the Holy Spirit and empowered to live on this earth!

Can you see?

- In the outer court God was cleansing us.

- In the holy place He is filling the clean vessel.

- In the outer court we are ready to die—in the holy place we are empowered to live and to draw near to God on earth!

Light is provided in the holy place for the priests to minister to the Lord by the power of the Holy Spirit, the Helper. Without the lampstand the priest would be unable to see to minister. The lampstand shows us that there is bread on the golden table of showbread. The lampstand reveals the golden altar where the priest worships and intercedes. The lampstand illuminates all of the activities in the holy place. When we walk in this light, we have fellowship with one another, as we read in 1 John 1:7a. There is a choice presented here— *if* we walk in the light. We can choose to walk in the light or choose not to.

The Holy Spirit knows how to glorify Jesus. He knows how to worship. When the believer begins to speak praises out of his mouth, the Holy Spirit ignites the praise that comes from our mouth, and the fire falls on his praise. Praise leads to the worship God seeks. The Holy Spirit pours the love of God into the worshipper's heart[114], and the worshipper has love to give back to God and to the people around him. The worshipper is enabled by God to love God with all his heart, soul, mind, and strength; he is enabled by God to love his neighbor as himself. God provides for us to give back to him—to do the first commandment: "Love the Lord your God with all your heart and with all your soul and with all your mind."[115] Like Mike Bickle says, "It takes God to love God." What an awesome God! Yay God! How can I but be a worshipper of God?

The Holy Spirit helps the believer give God what He seeks—worshippers that worship the Father in Spirit and truth; He helps the believer intercede, for we don't know how to pray as we should. The Holy Spirit helps us pray.

The Holy Spirit is God. God the Father and Jesus the Son are not jealous of the Holy Spirit. They are one, Father, Son, and Holy Spirit, and they always agree and work together in unity.

The Word of God commands us to be filled with the Holy Spirit in Ephesians 5:17–18. "Therefore do not be unwise, but understand what the will of the Lord is. And do not be drunk with wine, in which is dissipation; but be filled with the Spirit."

Here in the holy place, as we stop at the golden lampstand:

- We welcome the Holy Spirit
- We are filled with the Holy Spirit

- We are immersed in the Holy Spirit, surrounded by his illumination

There is no reason for the believer to be without help. When Jesus ascended to Father's right hand, he sent the promise of the Father, the gift of the Holy Spirit. Our Father provides everything we need—the gift of salvation through Jesus our Savior and the gift of the Holy Spirit. Make sure to ask for and receive the gift of the Holy Spirit.

Accept the invitation, come boldly to the throne of grace, and receive mercy and find grace! What a deal! Let's read Hebrews 4:16 again. "Let us therefore come boldly to the throne of grace, that we may obtain mercy and find grace to help in time of need." Mercy covers the past; grace gives you God's favor and ability for the future.

This is the holy place, and the Holy Spirit is available to help. Jesus said, "I will send a Helper just like me. I will come to you. [116]" The Helper has come—He came on Pentecost as we read in Acts chapter two. Jesus sent the promise of the Father.

Are we there yet?
Are we there yet? No, but we are making progress. The children of Israel were afraid to draw near,[117] and many times we too don't finish the journey. This is the holy place. It is the place closest to God, but He did not dwell there! This is the place where priests

fellowship. We are made holy by the righteousness of Jesus and the two cleansing agents. The blood of Jesus and the water of the Word of God keep us clean. The linen curtain of Jesus's righteousness surrounds us. We have help to finish the journey. O Holy Spirit, come fill me!

Let's pray:

Thank You, Lord, that You want me near You. Draw me close to You.

Thank You for making provision for me to come near to You.

Thank You that I can enter Your courts with thanksgiving in my heart.

Thank You for the blood of Jesus that gives me access into Your presence.

> *The blood has redeemed me—I have my sins forgiven.*
> *The blood has justified me—just as though I had never sinned.*
> *The blood of Jesus cleanses me from all sin as I walk in the light—hallelujah!*

Thank You for the Word of God that washes me.

Thank You that as I draw near to You, You draw near to me.

> *I want to come near—help me, Holy Spirit. Fill this clean vessel with the Spirit of God. Lord, I am asking, and I believe I will receive. When I ask for the Holy Spirit, You won't give me a stone or a serpent.[118] Fill me, Jesus.*

Immerse me in the Holy Spirit.
Thank you, Lord!

I want to get to know You, Holy Spirit, because You reveal Jesus. You reveal the way into the Holiest—into Father's presence! You reveal God—You are God! I love You, Holy Spirit. Amen.

CHAPTER 7

The Golden Table of Showbread— Jesus the Bread of Life

Our God is a mighty God. A person's first response to "mighty God" is often that of fear because God *is* so mighty. He is so awesome, so wonderful, so pure, so holy. This, the fear of the Lord, is the beginning of wisdom (Ps 111:10).The first requirement in drawing near to God is found in Leviticus 10:3; "By those who come near me I must be regarded as holy." The children of Israel were afraid of God's presence and did not draw near to Him. Let's read Exodus 20:18–21:

> Now all the people witnessed the thunderings, the lightning flashes, the sound of the trumpet, and the mountain smoking; and when the people saw it, they trembled and stood far off. Then they said to Moses, "You speak with us, and we will hear; but let not God speak with us, lest we die." And Moses said to the people, "Do not fear; for God has come to test you, and that His fear may be before you, so that you may not sin." So the

people stood afar off, but Moses drew near the thick darkness where God was.

There is a difference between being afraid of God and having the fear of God. Moses was able to move past the fear and draw near to God, but the children of Israel did not draw near. Let us also have the fear of God but not be afraid to draw near to Him.

It is the light from the golden lampstand that reveals the fourth stop on our journey: the golden table of showbread, which sat across from the lampstand. Exodus 40:22–24 describes the placement: "He put the table in the tabernacle of meeting, on the north side of the tabernacle, outside the veil; and he set the bread in order upon it before the LORD, as the LORD had commanded Moses. He put the lampstand in the tabernacle of meeting, across from the table."

What is the golden table of showbread? What is the showbread? Why do I need to make this stop?

The Golden Table of Showbread

The table of showbread was a small, ornately tooled table, sitting on the right side of the holy place, sparkling in the soft light of the lampstand. The description of the golden table of showbread is in Exodus 25:23–30:

You shall also make a table of acacia wood; two cubits shall be its length, a cubit its width, and a cubit and a half its height. And you shall overlay it with pure gold, and make a molding of gold all around. You shall make for it a frame of a handbreadth all around, and you shall make a gold molding for the frame all around. And you shall make for it four rings of gold, and put the rings on the four corners that are at its four legs. The rings shall be close to the frame, as holders for the poles to bear the table. And you shall make the poles of acacia wood, and overlay them with gold, that the table may be carried with them. You shall make its dishes, its pans, its pitchers, and its bowls for pouring. You shall make them of pure gold. And you shall set the showbread on the table before Me always.

The golden lampstand sits near the golden table of showbread and illuminates the table and the bread. The golden table of showbread was made according to the pattern given to Moses:

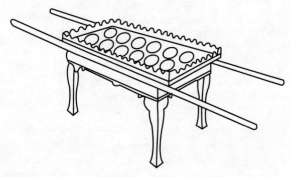

Golden Table of Showbread

- Made from acacia wood covered with pure gold
- Dimensions: three feet long, one and a half feet wide, and two and three–tenths feet high
- A gold rim encircled the top
- Two crowns of gold, to protect the bread
- Serving vessels of pure gold were placed upon it
- There were gold rings at each corner for the poles
- Poles were made of acacia wood covered with gold and used to transport the table

The Purpose of the Table

The main purpose of the table is to support the show-bread and to be the place of fellowship for priests to eat and drink before the Lord. This table, constructed by Spirit–filled craftsmen, is a place of communion—communion between the high priest and the other priests, between Jesus our High Priest and us who are his priesthood.

The table is for the bread. The priests fellow-shipped and ate at the table with one another in the light of the Holy Spirit. The communion table is the place we remember what Jesus has done for us. He is the table that holds the bread, and He is the bread on the table!

Judson Cornwall said in his book *Let Us Draw Near,*

> The primary purpose for this tabernacle is that
> God can have communion with man as He
> once had with Adam in the garden, with Noah
> and with Abraham. The table speaks of com-
> munion—a place to eat and drink before the
> Lord—the new wine and the bread of his face
> (presence).[119]

The Showbread

Placed upon the table were twelve loaves of unleavened bread. They were of equal size and weight and
arranged in two rows of six each. This was God's
bread[120] and the bread of the priests[121]—(God's bread,
for the priests).

> Word Study: *showbread,* Hebrew *paneh* (paw-
> neh'); Strong's #6440: the *face* (as the part that
> *turns*); used in a great variety of applications (lit.
> and fig.); also (with prep. pref.) as a prep. (*before,*
> etc.) So, we can say that showbread means *before
> the face* of God, or the bread that is before the
> face of God.

> Word Study: *showbread,* Hebrew *ma'areketh*
> (mah–ar–eh'–keth); Strong's #4635: an *arrange-
> ment,* i.e., (concr.) a *pile* (of loaves): –row,
> showbread.[122]

It was called showbread because the loaves of bread sat before the face or presence of God (who dwelt in the Holy of Holies) as a meal offering from the children of Israel.[123] Bread, the staff of life, represents strength. It is at this table eating this bread that we are strengthened in our spiritual life.

The showbread was, as stated in Leviticus 24:5–9:

- Made of fine flour
- Baked in the oven
- Placed fresh each Sabbath and sprinkled with frankincense for a memorial
- Eaten by Aaron and his sons (the priests) in the holy place

The showbread is freshly baked every six days and sprinkled with frankincense[124], a type of prayer, as a memorial. (We see frankincense throughout the holy place—sprinkled first on the bread and burned on the golden altar as an offering to God.[125] This is not the same incense that was prepared especially for the golden altar in Exodus 30:34–38. Frankincense is a fragrant gum resin with a silver–white cast. It was ground into powder and burned on the altar while the priest ate the showbread on the Sabbath.) The bread on the table had been placed there the week prior and had absorbed the presence of the Lord for seven days. This unleavened bread made from fine flour and baked in an oven was placed on the table close to God's presence for one week and then eaten by the priest. It is the Bread of His Presence.

In the old covenant the showbread foreshadowed Jesus Christ, the true bread of life. The bread was eaten each Sabbath by the priests, and twelve fresh loaves were put on the table to replace what had been eaten. In the new covenant Jesus is the true bread of life, giving strength to all who eat of Him.[126] The Word as food becomes part of an individual when the Word of God gets into his heart and becomes food for his inner man. He receives spiritual strength for worship and service just as the priests who ate the showbread did. Again, as with washing with the Word at the laver in the outer court, obedience is required—here at the table, as we eat the bread of life, the bread of His presence, we *do* the Word, and we are conformed into the image of Christ.[127]

Jesus, the Table

The table is symbolic of Jesus, Son of God and Son of Man: deity united. The table is made of acacia wood, which typifies Christ's humanity—Son of Man, then it is overlaid with pure gold, which speaks of His divine nature—Son of God.[128] This small, ornate table stood on the right side of the holy place and held the twelve loaves of showbread—the bread of His face.

In the old covenant, the golden table of showbread was an object, a type, of what was to come. The pattern was given to Moses in Exodus 25:23–30, as we have read. Every aspect of the table was a picture of the new covenant. In the new covenant, Jesus is the table—the place of communion, or fellowship. The acacia wood covered with pure gold was a type of Jesus. Acacia wood, picturing the humanity of Christ, is a hard, incorruptible, indestructible wood that grows in the Sinai Desert. The gold is a type of his deity. The golden table is a picture of His deity and humanity united. Jesus is the table that holds the bread; the bread is Jesus, the Bread of Life. In Christ lies our best example of the communion God desires to have with man: communion in Jesus and communion with Jesus, surrounded by Holy Spirit's illumination. This communion can't happen in natural light; we need supernatural illumination! It is at the table eating together that naturally reminds us of fellowship. It is at the Lord's table (1 Corinthians 10:21) that we find sweet fellowship with the other priests and our Great High Priest, Jesus. Jesus communes with us at the table, in sweet fellowship. Just as we invite a friend for lunch or coffee over a meal, He has called us into fellowship. "God is faithful, by whom you were called into the fellowship of His Son, Jesus Christ our Lord" (1 Corinthians 1:9). First John 1:7 says, "As we walk in the light as He is in the light, we have fellowship with one another." Also, "Behold, I stand at the door and knock. If anyone hears My voice and opens the door, I will come in to him and dine with him and he with Me" (Revelation 3:20). Jesus is asking for this fellowship! He is knocking. Do you hear His voice? I do. *O Jesus, come in and fellowship with me! I want to fellowship with You, Jesus. It is unbelievable that You want to fellowship with me!*

It is here at the golden table of showbread that we eat the Bread of Life; we partake of the bread and the wine; we have communion with Jesus, Holy Spirit, and with one another. This is the living bread that came down from heaven, John 6:51 tells us. As we eat the bread of life at the golden table, the nature of Jesus and our redeemed nature are blended and interwoven to create a whole new nature seen in the wood overlain with gold. The two are blended together. How does this happen? When we come to the table and eat the bread of communion, we become one with Jesus.[129] We agree with his Word, His will; we do what the Word says, we follow Jesus and become conformed to His image.[130] The true bread from heaven reveals to me who I am in Christ.

Jesus, the True Bread

Jesus alone is the true bread from God. In John 6:35, Jesus said, "I am the bread of life. He who comes to Me shall never hunger, and he who believes in me shall never thirst." And in John 6:51, "I am the living bread which came down from heaven. If anyone eats of this bread, he will live forever; and the bread that I shall give is My flesh, which I shall give for the life of the world." This bread is expensive, but Jesus paid for this meal!

The showbread is a type of Christ's sinless life. Made from fine flour, which was crushed, ground, and sifted, it shows us a picture of Jesus and his ministry and a picture of the believer who yields His will to the Word of God. As the believer yields, his will is ground, crushed, and sifted until it becomes even and uniform to God's Word.

Let's explore the meanings given us in the characteristics of the showbread:

- Made of fine flour (Leviticus 2:1)

    - Jesus was crushed, ground, sifted—by Satan (Matthew 4:4–11), by religious leaders (Matthew 22:15–40), yet without sin (Hebrews 4:15)

    - Jesus was beaten, scourged (Isaiah 53:4–5, Matthew 27:26–30)

    - Jesus was crucified for the sin of all men (Matthew 27:26–30)

The showbread was baked into loaves, which typifies the fire of trials, persecution, and His suffering death for us. The heat from the oven baked the loaves. Jesus experienced the fire of the oven, and we too know the fire of testing. First Peter 4:12–13 tells us: "Beloved, do not think it strange concerning the fiery trial which is to try you, as though some strange thing happened to you; but rejoice to the extent that you partake of Christ's sufferings, that when His glory is revealed, you may also be glad with exceeding joy." When we ask for God's fire, it is not just to keep us warm and cozy! The fire conforms us as well. The fire made the ingredients hold together; it's the fire that takes the cake batter and causes it to become that delicious cake! It is the same with us! We need God's fire!

The incense gave off a balsam–like fragrance that filled the holy place. Like frankincense, Jesus's life was fragrant. "Now thanks be to God who always leads us in triumph in Christ, and through us diffuses the fragrance of His knowledge in every place. For we are to God the fragrance of Christ among those who are being saved and among those who are perishing" (2 Corinthians 2:14–15). Jesus is the Bread of Life sprinkled with frankincense—a sweet fragrance, a wonderful aroma; when we pass through the trials of life yielding to Jesus, we produce a sweet aroma, pleasing to God. This is the place in our journey where we meet with the other priests in the holy place. We come to the table and fellowship with God and with one another, i.e., the priests who have come past the outer court. All of God's children may come into the holy place and eat at the table of showbread but for various reasons all don't:

1. A lack of knowledge[131]—they don't know they can go; they don't know it is available

2. A lack of progression—they have stopped on their journey

3. A lack of orientation—they thought they were already "there"

4. A lack of desire or vision—they stopped seeking

5. A lack of correct information—somebody told them they couldn't go; the traditions of man prevented them from going

6. A lack of boldness—they were afraid to go on

The Holy Place, a Place of Fellowship

The *koinonia,* or fellowship, is wonderful in the holy place. We have fellowship with the Holy Spirit, we have fellowship with Jesus, who is the Word, and we have fellowship with the other priests. In the holy place God gives us understanding of his Word. This is the Word illuminated by the Holy Spirit; the bread has been sitting in His presence for seven days! It has been soaking in the presence of God coming from the Holy of Holies! This is the bread of His presence!

Notice the involvement of the priests with the showbread: they made it (Leviticus 24:5–9); they put it on the table fresh each week; and only the priests ate the showbread. They ate the bread of His face, and it was life to them. We have access to the table of the Lord to commune and fellowship with Jesus, with Holy Spirit and with the priests. The Word becomes a part of us.

Just what does it mean to eat the bread of heaven? As we eat God's Word (not just hearing the Word but doing the Word), the bread of His presence, in the holy place, our lives are changed. When we come to Jesus, the table, and see the bread on the table, we have the opportunity to eat the bread of life—the showbread on the golden table. John 6:32–33, 35:

> Then Jesus said to them, "Most assuredly, I say to you, Moses did not give you the bread from heaven, but My Father gives you the true bread from heaven. For the bread of God is He who comes down from heaven and gives life to the world…I am the bread of life. He who comes to me shall never hunger, and he who believes in Me shall never thirst."

By making the Word a part of our lives, we are changed or conformed into the image of God. When we do the Word, it becomes a part of us, and we are changed as our minds are renewed. Our minds begin to align with God's way of thinking as we yield to the instruction in God's Word illuminated by the Holy Spirit.

As we eat the bread (the showbread that has been in the presence of God), we submit our wills to God's will. Our minds are being conformed to His. Our wills (as Jesus's was) must be ground into "fine flour"—there is a crushing of our wills as we are conformed to His image. I change my mind and give up my will and do what God's Word says. I *will* agree with Your Word, whether it is obeying my parents, being kind when I have been wronged, forgiving when I don't want to forgive, telling the truth when it is easier to deceive or lie about the situation, or saying no to sexual sins. Sometimes this is hot and fiery. The Holy Spirit is able to conform us to Jesus as we eat the Word and fellowship with the other priests. As we yield our will to His will and to His Word and "delight to do His will," His Spirit works in us. That work produces the will of God within us, and His Word becomes alive inside of us. We are progressing from the natural to the supernatural. We are on our way—we have the Helper! The Word, *logos*, becomes the Word, *rhema* to us. Logos is just black ink on white paper; rhema is when the word of God comes alive to me whether it is the written word or a word spoken by another person or even sometimes the word in a song. It is the anointed Word.

> Word Study: *word,* Greek *logos* (*log*–oss); Strong's #3056:[132] A transmission of thought, communication, a word of explanation, an utterance, discourse, divine revelation, talk, statement,

instruction, an oracle, divine promise, divine doctrine, divine declaration. Jesus is the living *logos* (John 1:1); the Bible is the written *logos* (Hebrews 4:12); and the Holy Spirit utters the spoken *logos* (I Corinthians 2:13).[133]

Word Study: word, Greek—*rhema* (*hray'*–mah): that which is or has been uttered by the living voice, thing spoken, word.[134] In other words, *rhema* is the living word, or the Word of God coming alive.

Here at the golden table I have the privilege of eating the Bread of Life. It is a decision, and I must decide to obey and do the Word of God. I set my will before the Lord. If my will does not agree with God's Word, guess who needs to change? When I make the decision to change my mind and agree with God's Word and do what it commands, I let my will become united with God's will. In this way my will is changed—ground, formed, and baked—and my will is conformed to God's will—i.e., I eat the Word of Life, and it becomes life within me.

Isaiah 55:10–11 tells us that the Word of God accomplishes God's purposes just like seed that is sown in the earth:

> For as the rain comes down, and the snow from heaven, and do not return there, but water the earth, and make it bring forth and bud, that it may give seed to the sower and bread to the eater,

so shall My word be that goes forth from My mouth; it shall not return to Me void, but it shall accomplish what I please, and it shall prosper in the thing for which I sent it.

In some seasons the Word of God is as rain, some seasons as snow. Snow and rain—better than fertilizer, but hard to receive. The ground is hard and frozen until the thaw comes. When you get a little warmer, it will melt and work in you. God's Word is accomplishing what He pleases in us; it is prospering in us, in the thing for which He sent it![135]

Renewing Our Minds

This transformation, this renewal of our minds, is spoken of in Romans 12:1–2.

I beseech you therefore, brethren, by the mercies of God, that you present your bodies a living sacrifice, holy, acceptable to God, which is your reasonable service. And do not be conformed to this world, but be transformed by the renewing of your mind, that you may prove what is that good and acceptable and perfect will of God.

We set our minds before God as we "do" His will. We set our wills before Him. Self–control is developed in us; we are not ruled by our emotions but by the Word of God. Many of us do not know how to control our emotions, but we *can* control our wills. Expose your will to God. Let your will go to the cross and die. You can decide to do this—you can choose. It is a decision to yield my will to God's will. You don't have to live by emotions. In exposing your will to God, you begin to exercise your will. You don't have to wait for the feelings. We have the bread of His face—it is set before Him twenty-four hours a day, seven days a week, day and night. God wants our will to be conformed to his Word twenty-four/seven. Our will must agree with His. Don't hold anything back, but surrender; give way to let God have *His* way in all that we are, all that we do—in our lives individually, in our marriages, in our children, in our church, in our ministries, in our occupations.

We need to deal with our minds, wills, and emotions (our souls) here, in the holy place, *so that* when we come to the golden altar (the next stop in our journey) our emotions don't dominate our spirit. Let the Holy Spirit come and fill every aspect of your mental life and possess it. Let your mind be illuminated and transformed, remembering this: God's Spirit never works apart from his Word. Psalm 33:6 reads, "By the word of the LORD the heavens were made, and all the host of them by the breath of His mouth." The breath of His mouth is his Spirit. In Genesis 1, the Spirit hovered, God spoke, and when the Word was united with the Spirit, there was light. When God's Word is united with His Spirit in your mind, there will be light.

Psalm 119:130 states, "The entrance of Your words gives light; it gives understanding to the simple." Can you sense God's Spirit hovering now as you are reading His Word written here? Just say, "Lord, let there be light in me!" And when the light goes on, it reveals the table of showbread. The Word of God will reveal the condition of our wills, and that's why some people don't want light. Light will reveal a rebellious will. But John 3:21 says: "But he who practices the truth comes to the Light, so that his deeds may be manifested as having been wrought in God."

It takes practice—just like working out or dieting. Work out every day! Practice coming to the light! I don't always trust my feelings; I don't walk by my feelings. My feelings may kiss me today and betray me tomorrow, but when my will is yielded, I can make a promise and keep it. When we are yielded to doing God's will and not to feelings, our lives are consistent—we are the same today and tomorrow.

Acting on the Word—My Story

After the Holy Spirit illuminated my life, I hungered for the bread of heaven, the bread of life; the Holy Spirit guided me to Jesus, the table, and I began to eat the bread of life. I learned the importance of acting on the Word of God from Gloria Copeland many years ago. Jesus gave the example of two men and how they responded after hearing the Word:

Therefore whoever hears these sayings of Mine, and does them, I will liken him to a wise man who built his house on the rock: and the rain descended, the floods came, and the winds blew and beat on that house; and it did not fall, for it was founded on the rock. But everyone who hears these sayings of Mine, and does not do them, will be like a foolish man who built his house on the sand: and the rain descended, the floods came, and the winds blew and beat on that house; and it fell. And great was its fall.

Matthew 7:24–27

"You make the decision which man you will be. You must decide! The wise man acted on the Word, and the foolish man mentally assented to the Word. You can be either man! Knowing what the Word says is not enough. You must act on that knowledge to get results. Both men heard the Word, and both houses experienced the storm; but the results were different. Acting on the Word put a foundation under the wise man's house that could not be moved, and his house suffered no loss. The foolish man who heard the Word but did not do it had no foundation when the floods came. His house may have been easier to build, but it had no power to stand. As truths are revealed to you in the Word, apply them to your circumstances and do them. You be the wise man that acts on the Word. When the adversities of life come against your house, it will stand because of the foundation of doing God's Word will make it stand. You will learn to act on the Word of God, just as you would the word of your doctor, lawyer, or best friend."[136]

Are you hungering for the bread of heaven? Is that your cry? Take time to tell Jesus right now.

The Bread of His Presence Gives the Life of God!

> Then Jesus said to them, "Most assuredly, I say to you, unless you eat the flesh of the Son of Man and drink His blood, you have no life in you. He who eats My flesh and drinks My blood abides in Me, and I in him. As the living Father sent Me, and I live because of the Father, so he who feeds on Me will live because of Me."
>
> John 6:53, 56–57

The Living Word of God has different purposes in different areas of our walk.

- At the laver—in the outer court—the Word washes

- At the table—in the holy place—the Word gives life

- At the mercy seat—in the Holy of Holies—we will find that the Word of God, the manna, gives revelation

We need the Word in every area of our lives. Man lives not by bread alone but by every word that proceeds from the mouth of God.[137] God's words are life! There is always bread on the table in the Father's house!

Coming to the table and participating and eating with the other priests is our privilege and responsibility. At this stop in our journey we must *eat* and *do* with others; *fellowship is not optional in our journey.* Here in the holy place we find the Holy Spirit to help us on our journey. He fills us and teaches us and leads us into all truth—to the table of God's Word—the Word filled with God's presence. No black ink on white paper here! The Holy Spirit illuminates and makes the Word alive—alive in me! We overflow as we are filled with the Holy Spirit and with God's Word, the bread of life.

God provides the bread of His presence to change us into His image and for fellowship with His body. When we come into the holy place, the Holy Spirit illuminates what is available for us. He is showing us the bread of God's face. I want to come to this table with you, fellow priest. I see the table that the Holy Spirit has revealed! I come to eat the bread of His presence so that I may be one with the Word of God, living by its strength, by its light. "Thy Word is a lamp unto my feet" (Psalm 119:105).

Summary

The golden table of showbread is an essential stop in our journey into the Holy of Holies. Again, we cannot continue without the showbread to feed us—supernatural food to grow us up and mature us! The showbread gives the life of Jesus to the believer. We *must* fellowship with the other priests who are there with us. Iron sharpening iron—don't run and hide! We are there for one another to lean on in hard times and to rejoice with in good times. We are not to journey alone. We are the family of God.[138] We gather to eat at God's table and fellowship with one another in the presence of the Holy Spirit's illumination, just as the priests did on the Sabbath day in the old covenant.

As we eat with the other priests, we help each other grow and mature. We nurture one another, and even "sharpen" one another as stated in Proverbs 27:17: "As iron sharpens iron, so a man sharpens the countenance of his friend." Sometimes we want to stay apart, but we are not made to be alone. The priests ate at the table together and fellowshipped together in the holy place. When we fellowship with our fellow priests in the holy place, the Holy Spirit illuminates the table, where the Word of God is, and brings light to our minds. Our minds change as we do, or "eat," the Word of God.

Jesus is the table—earthly and divine, Son of Man and Son of God—made of wood, representing earth but covered with pure gold. We come to this table, the one who holds the bread that has absorbed the presence of God, the showbread, the Word of God. Jesus Christ is both the sustainer—the table and the substance—the bread, of the fellowship that we believer priests have with the Father. He is the table and the bread of that table. Fellowship in Christ with fellow priests is God's provision at the golden table of showbread.

The golden table of showbread is a wonderful place. Many want to stop the journey here; they think they have arrived—they are full of the Holy Spirit, eating the bread of heaven, fellowshipping with the other priests. Don't separate yourself from the body of communion and fellowship. It will hinder your journey. Draw near to God, and you will draw nearer to those who are drawing near.

Are we there yet?

Are we there yet? No, but we are on our way. We are clean, made holy by the blood of Jesus and washed by the water of His Word in the outer court. We are illuminated—filled by the Holy Spirit, and we are eating—fellowshipping with the Holy Spirit, Jesus, and the other priests. But remember our destination is the mercy seat, God's dwelling place. The closer we draw, the more of His presence we feel. But we are not there yet! Judson Cornwall understood this and wrote about it in the epilogue of his book, *Let Us Draw Near.* He showed us how the pattern of the Tabernacle of Moses has been revealed to the body of Christ during the last four hundred years. It has been a process and it has been progressive and it reveals where we are presently as the body of Christ. God is calling us to get up from the table and pray and intercede and come into His presence. This is how Judson Cornwall said it:

> The light of God had nearly gone out during the Middle Ages. When God revealed to Martin Luther in the early sixteenth century the electrifying truth, "The just shall live by his faith" (Habakkuk 2:4), within a few years the ministry of the brazen altar was restored to the church, but not without great persecution.
>
> In the eighteenth century the Wesley brothers' dynamic preaching of sanctification set the stage for the ministry of the laver. Although their message was rejected at first and they paid a great price—the church now had a complete Outer Court. For nearly a hundred years the church contented herself in the outer court.
>
> But…at the beginning of the twentieth century, God again visited his church with an outpouring of his Spirit that stirred the religious world, and the ministry of the Candlestick was relearned and returned to the church. Rejection and reprisals slowly forced these Spirit–baptized saints out of their fundamental churches to form the Pentecostal denomination. Somehow at each stop or move of the Spirit we think we've got

"it"—we think we are "there"—we have attained the ultimate in relationship with God. But even with this outpouring of the Holy Spirit, in fact only the first station in the holy place was being restored to the church. God still wanted a more intimate relationship with his people.

The Charismatic Renewal again brought an outpouring of the Holy Spirit. Fellowship and great teaching have been emphasized. Denominational walls have been ignored as Spirit–filled believers gathered in conferences and prayer meetings just to enjoy Jesus and each other. The Table of Shewbread has been once more in place in the church.

Do you see how each article from the tabernacle has been restored to the body of Christ? First, when Martin Luther received the revelation that restored the brazen altar. Two centuries later when the Wesley brothers' emphasis of the Word restored the brazen laver. And another two centuries later, in 1906, the Holy Spirit was poured out at Azusa Street, and the lampstand burned once more. Then the teaching of the 1970's returned the table of showbread.

This was in 1977. Now we see the Holy Spirit's emphasis in prayer, intercession, and worship, which is the golden altar—our next stop. We can see into the Holy of Holies because Jesus tore the veil away. We can see in, but we aren't there yet! We are looking for the presence more than presents. We want to see your face, Jesus. Draw us close to you. Do you see the process? Do you know where you are? Come boldly covered by the blood of Jesus and enter on in.

There is one more article of furniture in the holy place. It is the golden altar. Let's continue on our journey and visit the golden altar before we enter the Holy of Holies where God's presence dwells!

Let's pray:
Thank You, Father, for the bread of heaven, your provision for me.
I thank You that I can come and be filled here in the holy place.
I thank You for the fellowship to which You have called me.
I love the table, Jesus, and the bread of His face, but help me not to get too satisfied here.
I love the fellowship with Jesus and the other priests.
I know I'm not there yet, and I can hear You calling me to draw nearer.
I will come, Lord.
I will obey the Your voice and follow where the Holy Spirit leads.

I love You, Jesus. You are my King! Amen.

CHAPTER 8

The Golden Altar of Incense—
Worship and Intercession

Our hearts are set on getting to our destination. It is hard to get up from the table and move to the altar, but Ecclesiastes 7:8 states: "The end of a thing is better than its beginning." We are not there yet! Can you hear Holy Spirit calling out, "There is more"? We have come out of the outer court into the holy place where the light from the golden lampstand reveals the golden lampstand, the golden table of showbread, and the golden altar of incense. We have stopped at the lampstand and the table. The next stop is the golden altar of incense.

In the holy place we learn to let the Holy Spirit lead us. Romans 8:14 tells us, "For as many as are led by the Spirit of God, these are sons of God." Have you decided to press in, to continue the journey into God's presence? Sometimes it is hard to leave the food and fellowship at the table and make this move to give at the altar. We are no longer looking to just get something from God; we aren't just looking for the blessings—we are seeking God for who He is. God's hand, full of blessing, has reached out to us and is drawing us near. We have come to minister to Him, to draw near to Him. We have come to worship Him, not only for what He does but because He is worthy to be worshipped. We seek your face, O God of Jacob.[139]

Our hearts are full:

- Of the Holy Spirit
- Of the bread of His presence, the showbread
- Of the fellowship of other believer priests

But remember, the Father's purpose in all of this is to have us with Him. Jesus came to bring us to Father. Let's not stop now.

Here in the holy place, God pours his love in our hearts. Romans 5:5b states: "The love of God has been poured out in our hearts by the Holy Spirit who was given to us." We have God's love in us to give back to Him! Isn't that awesome! God gives us His love to give back to Him and to those around us! He is the One who *enables* us to do the first commandment—to "love the LORD your God with all your heart, with all your soul, and with all your mind and with all your strength," and the second commandment as well, "You shall love your neighbor as yourself."[140]

The Holy Spirit has poured love in our hearts so that we can give love back to God and so that we can love our neighbor as ourselves. *If* we have been doing the Word and practicing what we have learned, we have been eating the bread of His face, and we are approaching the golden altar where the Holy Spirit helps us pray and worship. We don't know how to pray as we ought, but we have help![141]

Do you feel inadequate when it comes to worship and prayer? I guess we all do, but God has made provision here, at the altar, the place of sacrifice! Our Great High Priest, Jesus, is our teacher who teaches us to pray, and the Holy Spirit is here to illuminate—to show us the altar and to help us pray! The Holy Spirit helps us worship. The Holy Spirit represents the fire of God, and just as the fire on the altar causes the incense to give off a sweet aroma to God, the fire of the Holy Spirit releases the fragrance of our prayers and worship!

Our hearts are overflowing. Will we priests just overflow on ourselves and on one another? No, we want to give; and now we have something to give:

- Worship—to Father
- Intercession—to those in need as we pray alongside our Great High Priest, Jesus.

We come to the golden altar of incense with the intent of worshipping and interceding. We are aware of the choice we are making: an altar is a place of sacrifice. It will cost us something even though we are giving back what God has given to us. Under the new covenant, the new and living way, the priest ministers to the Lord with worship and intercession at the golden altar, the fifth stop in our journey and the third piece of furniture in the holy place.

The Golden Altar—the Smallest Piece of Furniture in Tabernacle

The description of the golden altar is found in Exodus 30:1–10. The golden altar of incense is the smallest article of furniture in the tabernacle; it is much smaller than the brazen altar, which is seven feet square. The altar of incense is thirty–six inches high and eighteen inches square.

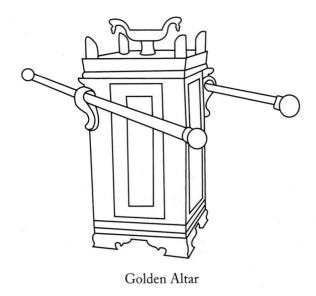

Golden Altar

The altar was made of acacia wood overlaid with gold in contrast to the brass of the large brazen altar. It had horns at each corner, also made of gold. The horns of the altar served a specific purpose in relationship to the blood sacrifice. On the Day of Atonement (the tenth day of the seventh month), the high priest took some of the blood that was to be used to sprinkle the mercy seat and applied it to the altar to "make atonement upon its horns" (Exodus 30:10). (The blood applied to our intercession makes it effective!) The altar served as a place of recompense (payment) for the sins of the priests and the congregation.[142] A gold rim encircled the top of the altar with gold rings at each corner for the gold–covered acacia wood poles used to transport it.

God told Moses to place the altar in front of the veil[143] that separated the holy place from the Holy of Holies where God's presence dwelt. The golden altar was the closest the priest could come to the presence of God under the old covenant.

As the priest approached the golden altar, he took a censer (a container in which incense is burned) full of burning coals from the brazen altar in one hand and specially prepared sweet incense in the other and carried it inside the first veil. The incense was a precise mixture of three specific sweet perfumes mixed with frankincense.[144] They produce a sweet aroma when placed on hot coals of the censer—a sweet aroma to

God. The coals from the censer were placed on the golden altar, and the incense was sprinkled over the burning coals.[145] The same fire that consumed the sacrifice on the brazen altar consumes the incense. This created a thick cloud of smoke that filled the tabernacle and symbolized Israel's prayers to God.[146] The incense was to be burned perpetually before the Lord.[147]

Incense was offered at regular times.[148] The priest offered morning and evening sacrifices on the brazen altar and then entered the holy place to trim the lamps and to burn incense on the golden altar.[149]

The priest, before offering the incense, had first met the requirements. In order to do so, he:

- had ministered at the brazen altar (the first cleansing agent, the blood)
- had washed at the brazen laver (the second cleansing agent, the water)
- had entered the holy place
  - and been filled with the Holy Spirit
  - and fellowshipped and eaten God's bread with the other priests

The priest took a censer full of burning coals and sprinkled the specially prepared sweet incense over them. He is now offering worship and intercession here at the golden altar.

In the old covenant the priests could go no farther than the holy place. The golden altar was located just in front of the veil that separated the holy place from the Holy of Holies. The priests could not see into the Holy of Holies. Only the high priest could enter the Holy of Holies—only once each year on the Day of Atonement.[150] The priests ministered at the golden altar at the time of the morning and evening sacrifice.

Ministering at the Golden Altar— the Hour of Prayer

Great things happen at regular times—the appointed times of prayer, which were morning and evening sacrifices. Let's look at examples of what happened in the lives of men of God in the Bible at the time of the evening sacrifice, the hour of prayer. All of these happened at the same time that the priest was ministering at this altar in the tabernacle.

- Elijah: 1 Kings 18:36, 38—"And it came to pass, *at the time of the offering of the evening sacrifice,* that Elijah the prophet came near and said, 'LORD God of Abraham, Isaac, and Israel, let it be known this day that You are God in Israel and I am Your servant, and that I have done all these things at Your word.' Then the fire of the LORD fell and consumed the burnt sacrifice" (emphasis added).

- Daniel: Daniel 9:21—"Yes, while I was speaking in prayer, the man Gabriel, whom I had seen in the vision at the beginning, being caused to fly swiftly, reached me *about the time of the evening offering*" (emphasis added).

- Peter and John: Acts 3:1–10—"Now Peter and John went up together to the temple *at the hour of prayer*, the ninth hour. And a certain man lame from his mother's womb was carried, whom they laid daily at the gate of the temple which is called Beautiful, to ask alms from those who entered the temple; who, seeing Peter and John about to go into the temple, asked for alms. And fixing his eyes on him, with John, Peter said, 'Look at us.' So he gave them his attention, expecting to receive something from them. Then Peter said, 'Silver and gold I do not have, but what I do have I give you: In the name of Jesus Christ of Nazareth, rise up and walk.' And he took him by the right hand and lifted him up, and immediately his feet and ankle bones received strength. So he, leaping up, stood and walked and entered the temple with them—walking, leaping, and praising God. And all the people saw him walking and praising God. Then they knew that it was he who sat begging alms at the Beautiful Gate of the temple; and they were filled with wonder and amazement at what had happened to him" (emphasis added).

- Cornelius: Acts 10:30–31—"So Cornelius said, 'Four days ago I was fasting until this hour; and *at the ninth hour* I prayed in my house, and behold, a man stood before me in bright clothing, and said, "Cornelius, your prayer has been heard, and your alms are remembered in the sight of God"'" (italics mine).

- Zacharias: Luke 1:1:10–13—"And the whole multitude of the people was praying outside *at the hour of incense.* Then an angel of the Lord appeared to him (Zacharias), standing on the right side of the altar of incense…The angel said to him, 'Do not be afraid, Zacharias, for your prayer is heard; and your wife Elizabeth will bear you a son, and you shall call his name John'" (emphasis added).

- Jesus: Matthew 27:45–51—"Now from the sixth hour until the ninth hour there was darkness over all the land. And *about the ninth hour* Jesus cried out with a loud voice, saying, 'Eli, Eli, lama sabachthani?' that is, 'My God, My God, why have You forsaken Me?'…Then, behold, the veil of the temple was torn in two from top to bottom; and the earth quaked, and the rocks were split" (Emphasis added).

- Prayers of the saints: that's you and me! Revelation 8:3–4—"Then another angel, having a golden censer, came and stood at the altar. He was given much incense, that he should offer it with the prayers of all the saints upon the golden altar which was before the throne. And the smoke of the incense, with the prayers of the saints, ascended before God from the angel's hand."

- Me! Psalm 141:2—"Let my prayer be set before You as incense, The lifting up of my hands as the evening sacrifice."

Each of these events took place as the priest was ministering at the golden altar. This encourages me to pray and worship and minister to the Lord, i.e. sacrifice, prayer and worship. It will probably cost me something—time!

A warning is given us concerning the type of incense or fire used on the golden altar in worship—no strange incense, no strange fire—or the penalty is death. Let us look at Exodus 30:7 regarding the incense: "Aaron shall burn on it sweet incense every morning; when he tends the lamps, he shall burn incense on it. You shall not offer strange incense on it," and Leviticus 6:13, 16:12 regarding the fire taken from the brazen altar to the altar of incense: "*A fire shall always be burning on the altar; it shall never go out.* Then he shall take a censer full of burning coals of fire from the altar before the LORD, *with his hands full of sweet incense* beaten fine, and bring it inside the veil" (emphasis added).

We see the blood and fire in each part of the tabernacle. This is a type of how we need the blood of Jesus and the Holy Spirit to take us into the presence of God. We can't get there in our own righteousness (hence the blood) or by our own power or enlightenment (hence the Holy Spirit). God has made all provision for us to enter in to his presence. He makes us holy.[151] At the golden altar, we are approaching—drawing near—to the throne of God. We have gotten this far by the blood of Jesus, the Word of God, and the illumination of the Holy Spirit; don't start trusting in your flesh now! God's command is to keep the wood on the fire and the prayer on the altar. That is a challenge. Let's obey.

Two Altars in the Tabernacle

The first altar, the brazen altar in the outer court, was for man. Everything that needed to be accomplished there was done for man—God did it for him. But here in the holy place, at the golden altar, the priest offers the sacrifice—worshipping God and interceding for others.

> Word Study: *altar, mizbeach* (meez–*beh*–ahch); Strong's #4196:[152] Altar, place of sacrifice. The root of *mizbeach* is *zabach*, which means "to slay, to sacrifice, to offer an animal." The word *mizbeach* occurs more than 400 times. Altars were of great importance in the lives of Noah and the

three patriarchs. In the Levitical system and in Solomon's temple, the altar was the center of daily activity, without which the rest of Israel's worship could not take place. The "altar of sacrifice" was also crucial in God's revelation of true worship for joyful times, such as feasts.[153]

Let's compare the purposes and characteristics of the two altars:

Brazen Altar	Altar of Incense
• Large—seven feet square	• Small—eighteen inches square
• Made of brass, which typified sin/judgment	• Made of gold, which typifies Christ's deity
• Meets man's need to be delivered from sin	• Provides for the worshipper to worship God and intercede for others in order for God's purposes to come to pass on earth
• Purpose is for receiving from God	• Purpose is for giving to God
• Is available to "whosoever"	• Available for priests only to minister to God
• Located outside	• Located inside
• A place of suffering, typifying Christ as Savior	• A place of worship and intercession, typifying Jesus our great intercessor
• We come here as sinners	• We come as saints—we are saints, the righteousness of God in Christ

The two altars have different functions.

- The brazen altar meets man's need to be saved from sin
- The golden altar of incense gives man a way and a place to worship and minister to God

We are at the second altar, another place of transition: the golden altar is *in* the holy place, but it is *for* the Holy of Holies, giving a way to access the entrance of the Holy of Holies. The golden altar is the place where I give worship and intercession with the help of the Holy Spirit. Our clean vessels are full of the Holy Spirit. We have eaten Christ at the golden table, and we are full and ready to give back to God. This is where the priest can minister to God; worshipping and interceding as we enter the presence of God.

Let us not get the two altars confused. The brazen altar in the outer court is for the purpose of dealing with sin and sacrifice for salvation. It takes care of man's needs. The golden altar in the holy place is the place of worship and intercession. We begin to want what God wants, and we begin to listen for what he wants us to ask for in prayer. At the golden altar we are seeing Christ the person, not his work. I want to agree with you, Jesus. Let your kingdom come! Let your will be done on earth! In me, in my marriage, in my family! In the church where you have placed me! In the state where I live! In the nations of the world! Rule and reign King Jesus! Lead on O King Eternal!

Are we there yet? No. The golden altar is the last article of furniture we encounter before entering the Holy of Holies—the presence of God. It is transitional, where praise becomes worship and prayer becomes intercession. It is where incense is offered, a sweet fragrance to God.

"And you shall put it before the veil that is before the ark of the Testimony, before the mercy seat that is over the Testimony, *where I will meet with you*" (Exodus 30:6, emphasis added).

Symbolic of Jesus

The golden altar typifies Jesus, our great High Priest and intercessor; we are joining Him to intercede for others, and our hearts long to have them make this journey with us. We want our spouses, our children, and our friends and loved ones enjoying this feast with us. We are finding our hearts satisfied, and we know others that we want to have this peace and to know God—His presence. Even as I write this, I sense a prayer rise up inside of me. *O, Father, as a priest unto God, I apply the blood of Jesus to the horns of the altar for*

(insert names). Draw them close to You. Let them experience the communion of the saints with the Lord. Have mercy, my King.

Seeing then that we have a great High Priest who has passed through the heavens, Jesus the Son of God, let us hold fast our confession. For we do not have a High Priest who cannot sympathize with our weaknesses, but was in all points tempted as we are, yet without sin. Let us therefore come boldly to the throne of grace so that we may obtain mercy and find grace to help in time of need.

Hebrews 4:14–16

We…have strong consolation, who have fled for refuge to lay hold of the hope set before us. This hope we have as an anchor of the soul, both sure and steadfast, and which enters the presence behind the veil, where the forerunner has entered for us, even Jesus, having become High Priest forever.

Hebrews 6:18b–20

Jesus has become a surety of a better covenant…because he continues forever, has an unchangeable priesthood. Therefore he is also able to save to the uttermost those who come to God through Him, since He always lives to make intercession for them. For such a High Priest was fitting for us, who is holy, harmless, undefiled, separate from sinners, and has become higher than the heavens; who does not need daily, as those high priests, to offer up sacrifices, first for his own sins and then for the people's, for this He did once for all when He offered up himself. For the law appoints as high priests men who have weakness, but the word of the oath, which came after the law, appoints the Son who has been perfected forever. Now this is the main point of the things we are saying: We have such a High Priest, who is seated at the right hand of the throne of the Majesty in the heavens, a Minister of the sanctuary and of the true tabernacle which the Lord erected, and not man.

Hebrews 7:22, 24–28; 8:1–2

Hallelujah! Hallelujah! Hallelujah!

We have a great High Priest fitted for us. He fits me! He is a priest forever! He is the forerunner. He has gone before me and entered the presence! He has become *my* High Priest forever. What a glorious provision Father has given. No wonder I can come with boldness and enter God's presence. I have a great High Priest to take me in!

"And the Word became flesh and dwelt among us, and we beheld His glory, the glory as of the only begotten of the Father, full of grace and truth" (John 1:14). Humanity and deity wedded into one person— the God of the universe became flesh, like sinful man, for the purpose of giving His life's blood in order for our sins to be forgiven and so that we could come into fellowship with the Father.

"Christ loved the church and gave Himself for her so that:

- He might sanctify and cleanse her with the washing of water by the word

- He might present her to Himself a glorious church, not having spot or wrinkle or any such thing

- But that she should be holy and without blemish"

Ephesians 5:25b–27

"Christ hath redeemed us:

- That the blessing of Abraham might come upon the Gentiles in Christ Jesus

- That we might receive the promise of the Spirit through faith"

Galatians 3:13–14

What a Savior! God became man to reconcile man to God. Jesus gives us access into God's presence. He is our golden altar! Each stop is taking us closer, and as we approach the Holy of Holies we sense God's presence more and more. He is drawing us. We are drawing near the throne of grace to find mercy and to receive grace.[154]

In the new covenant, the Word became flesh and dwelt among us, as stated in John 1:14. Jesus became our altar, the golden altar of incense, which symbolized daily prayer to God. This altar is a type of Christ as our intercessor.

Made of acacia wood overlaid with pure gold, this altar typifies Christ's humanity and deity becoming one. Acacia wood and gold always typify the God–man, earth and heaven brought to us by Jesus.

The high priest took the incense into the Holy of Holies in his censer. Worship at this altar is the last act of the believer/priest before entering the Holy of Holies, God's presence. We will enter God's presence with worship—the censer of incense—and prayer.

Prayer at the golden altar:

- Is concerned more with God than people. It is more praise than petition; it is more about blessing God than asking for things.

- Declares that the one seated on heaven's throne is to be exalted above all things. At this altar, God is ministered to. This is what Revelation 5:8 is talking about; "The four living creatures and the twenty–four elders fell down before the Lamb, each having a harp, and golden bowls full of incense, which are the prayers of the saints."

- Is the prayer of adoration and intercession that declares God's Word on earth—

"Your kingdom come. Your will be done on earth as it is in heaven" (Luke 11:2). Lord, fill the earth with your glory! Have your way, King of kings and Lord of lords! Rule in the midst of your enemies! Hallelujah! Amen!

The High Priest has brought the *blood from the brazen altar* to sprinkle on the horns of the golden altar. At the brazen altar, the priest has all he needs to enter the Holy of Holies since Jesus, our forerunner, has made the way. The priest has brought *fire from the brazen altar* to light the lampstand and light the fire in the golden altar. The fire in his censer caused the incense to produce a sweet fragrance before the Lord. Our prayer in the new covenant is the incense, and we are the sweet fragrance. "For we are to God the fragrance of Christ among those who are being saved and among those who are perishing" (2 Corinthians 2:15).

The Offering for the Altar

The golden altar was made for the sweet incense of prayer and intercession.

Remember, the altar was made for sweet incense[155], not strange incense. The incense was offered every morning and every evening. Judson Cornwall, in his book *Let Us Draw Near,* wrote, "All incense 'worship' must be burned on the Golden Altar (Christ Jesus) if it is ever to come into God's presence, for only this altar is positioned in front of the veil only a few feet from the mercy seat of God" (p.130). Jesus is shown in every article of furniture—the same person not the same purpose. He is the golden altar, and there I offer my sacrifice of praise. "Let my prayer be set before You as incense, the lifting up of my hands as the evening sacrifice" (Psalm 141:2). We are a sweet aroma to God, the prayers of the saints upon the golden altar which ascend before God (Revelation 8:3–4, paraphrased).

Here, our eyes are being turned from what God *does* to who God *is*. At the golden altar, our concern is with the desire of God, not man. As the prayer and praise come from the worshipper, God is worshipped, and man is affected by that worship.

He has redeemed us to be seated with Him, to rule with Him as his bride. He is equipping us to rule and reign with Him. Our destiny is the throne! We are seated with Christ! "If then you were raised with Christ, seek those things which are above, where Christ is, sitting at the right hand of God. Set your mind on things above, not on things on the earth. For you died, and your life is hidden with Christ in God" (Colossians 3:1–3)!

God's Provision—the Helper

Don't we all feel inadequate to pray—to intercede? God has made provision! He didn't intend for us to be without him to help! As a priest, I too need to come to Jesus.

- At the cross, the brazen altar
- To the Word, the brazen laver
- To be filled with the Holy Spirit, golden lampstand
- To eat and fellowship, the golden table of showbread

Then I am ready to worship. God provides for His purpose to be fulfilled. He gives us what we need in order to minister to Him at the golden altar. He has made provision—He is Jehovah Jireh, our provider. He provides the sacrifice for the altar!

The golden altar is in the holy place, where the Holy Spirit helps us pray and worship. We need help to pray and to worship. The question is, will we ask for help and receive the Helper?

- The Holy Spirit knows how to pray and intercede—Romans 8:26
- He knows how to glorify Jesus—John 16:14
- He knows what is in Father's mind—1 Corinthians 2:10 states, "But God has revealed them [his mysteries] to us through the Holy Spirit. For the Spirit searches all things, yes, the deep things of God."

- The Holy Spirit reveals God's secrets, unveils God's mysteries—1 Corinthians 2:12: "Now we have received, not the spirit of the world, but the Spirit who is from God, that we might know the things that have been freely given to us by God."

- He helps us pray out God's plans and purposes— Romans 8:26

- He gives ability to our desire to worship—He knows how, and He knows what pleases Father—1 Corinthians 2:9–13

The Holy Spirit is illuminating the golden altar in the holy place to help us pray and worship; and Jesus, our great High Priest, is here to intercede with us. Repeating what we are told in Hebrews 4:14–16: "Seeing then that we have a great High Priest who has passed through the heavens, Jesus the Son of God, let us hold fast our confession. For we do not have a High Priest who cannot sympathize with our weaknesses, but was in all points tempted as we are, yet without sin." Here the invitation is issued: "Let us therefore *come boldly* to the throne of grace, that we may obtain mercy and find grace to help in time of need" (emphasis added). We can agree with God—now, how good is that? And we can worship! The Holy Spirit testifies of Jesus; He knows how to help us worship! Holy Spirit worships Jesus through me!

Now, we know that the Holy Spirit knows how to pray (intercede), for in Romans 8:26–27 we read:

> Likewise the Spirit also helps us in our weaknesses. For we do not know what we should pray for as we ought, but the Spirit Himself makes intercession for us with groanings which cannot be uttered. Now He who searches the heart knows what the mind of the Spirit is, because He makes intercession for the saints according to the will of God.

We have help to intercede! Hallelujah! We have the Holy Spirit and Jesus our great intercessor—what provision! I think people have such a hard time worshipping and interceding we really need to know that the Holy Spirit wants to pray with and through us and that Jesus is our great teacher in prayer.

At the golden altar we join our heavenly intercessor Jesus as we intercede and worship. This is where we can join with Jesus as He sings over us.[156] Jesus says in Hebrews 2:12: "I will declare Your name to My brethren; in the midst of the assembly I will sing praise to You." So, we can "by Him let us continually offer the sacrifice of praise to God, that is, the fruit of our lips, giving thanks to His name" (Hebrews 13:15). Jesus is here to assist us with prayer and praise, as is the Holy Spirit. We need not rely on our inadequacy! We need only to ask for help! Here we are focused on what God wants. Even as the fragrance of Mary's perfume filled the room when she anointed Jesus' feet,[157] the fragrance of our prayer and worship fills the room and penetrates the clothing so that we smell good to God! The incense gets on us and causes us to smell like Jesus—a sweet fragrance.

When we leave the secret place of God's presence, we should have the fragrance of the incense offered at the Golden Altar on us. Worshippers bring the fragrance of God into all the places they go! We will be just like Mary—her hair smelled just like Jesus's perfumed feet. God's purpose and desire for a kingdom of priests is fulfilled in us! We have a great High Priest who has gone before us. Second Peter 2:5 says, "You also, as living stones, are being built up a spiritual house, a holy priesthood, *to offer up spiritual sacrifices* acceptable to God through Jesus Christ" (emphasis added) He has made me into an overflowing worshipper.

A Seeking God

God is seeking worshippers and intercessors. Because of His provision for us we can give Him what he seeks! God seeks:

- Intercessors—Ezekiel 22:30: "So I sought for a man among them who would make a wall, and stand in the gap before Me on behalf of the land, that I should not destroy it; but I found no one."

Isaiah 59:1: "He saw that there was no man, and wondered that there was no intercessor."

- Worshippers—John 4:23–24: "But the hour is coming, and now is, when the true worshipers will worship the Father in spirit and truth; for the Father is seeking such to worship Him. God is Spirit, and those who worship Him must worship in spirit and truth."

Intercession and worship minister to God; intercessors and worshippers are what God seeks. Intercession and worship are priestly ministries. We do the work of the priest in the holy place before we rule as kings with Jesus in the Holy of Holies.

Here at the golden altar we can satisfy God's heart! How awesome the Holy Spirit is. He is the one who knows how to testify of Jesus and to glorify Him. We have the help we need to worship and intercede. Jesus gave us the Helper.

We draw near to the throne of grace to receive mercy and find grace to help! We receive mercy, which takes care of our past—our sins are blotted out, and we find grace; God's grace gives us his ability for the future—all power! Second Corinthians 9:8 says, "God is able to make all grace abound toward you, that you, always having all sufficiency in all things."

We are in the holy place. As we eat the bread and fellowship with fellow priests, the Holy Spirit draws us to worship and pray. We have the help we need to worship and pray.

My Story

I had been baptized in the Holy Spirit for over twenty years, and I had been in God's presence many times when I began to hunger for more of God and to seek His face. David said it so beautifully in Psalm 27:4–5. "One thing I have desired of the LORD, that will I seek: that I may dwell in the house of the LORD all the days of my life, to behold the beauty of the LORD, and to inquire in his temple."

As I mentioned earlier, I was teaching the Pentateuch in Community Bible Study. In Exodus 25:21–22 God told Moses,

> You shall put the mercy seat on top of the ark, and in the ark you shall put the Testimony that I will give you. And there I will meet with you, and I will speak with you from above the mercy seat, from between the two cherubim which are on the ark of the Testimony, about everything which I will give you in commandment to the children of Israel.

I thought, *I've got to find out how to get to the mercy seat!*

When I attended the Brownsville Revival in Pensacola, Florida, a new change began in me. I heard the song, "Come Running to the Mercy Seat," and a passion for the heavenly bridegroom was imparted to me. It was like a seed that began to grow, and passion for the heavenly bridegroom grew inside my heart. I began to seek God with a new intensity. I knew Hebrews 4:16 well: "Let us therefore come boldly to the throne of grace, that we may obtain mercy and find grace to help in time of need." I began to pour over Andrew Murray's *The Holiest of All*, and I began to *do* Hebrews 10:19. I began to enter by faith into the Holiest by the blood of Jesus, because I saw the invitation/command. He said I could, so I came. As I continued to come I saw the pattern! Do you see it too? It is God's revelation! In the presence of the Lord there is fullness of joy—here my heart is satisfied. I have never been the same. I have found what my soul has longed for in God's presence. I am learning how to dwell, how to abide, in the secret place. Thank you, Lord, for your wonderful provision.

Are we there yet?

Where are you? Are you still at the table? Are you beginning to minister to the Lord in worship and intercession? Are you hungry to pursue God? Are you crying, "Open the eyes of my heart, Lord. I want to see You"? The Holy Spirit is illuminating the golden altar. Are you "having boldness to enter the Holiest by the blood of Jesus, by the new and living way"? Enter in. Father has made all provision! Accept the invitation (Hebrews 4:16), draw near—enter boldly (Hebrews 10:19). *There is a difference in drawing near the Throne of Grace and entering the Holy of Holies.* You can draw near the White House but never enter the Oval Office of the President of the United States. We are invited to enter into the King of Kings's chambers. His blood and the water of the Word make us holy, and the Holy Spirit illuminates the way. Come on—enter boldly!

We can see our destination—but we are not there yet. The Holy Spirit is in charge of getting us into the Holy of Holies.[158] Jesus opened the way—the Holy Spirit is in charge of entry. As we draw nearer, we have the invitation to enter in. When you feel inadequate, ask the Holy Spirit to help. This is God's idea—His plan; He wants us in His presence. We have boldness to enter—can we ever be content to just draw near? It would be like having an invitation to my house and coming to the front door but not ever coming in! We are invited not only to draw near the throne of grace, but we are invited to come boldly into the Holiest. Is that a command? I think so.

Let's pray:
Draw me closer to Your heart;
Draw me close to You.
My heart is longing for Your chambers…
I seek your holy habitation, Lord.[159]

Oh, Jesus, you have brought me to Father.
You are the Way, the Truth, and the Life.
Draw me close to You.
Holy Spirit, help me enter boldly into the Holiest of all.
Amen.

CHAPTER 9

The Holy of Holies—Entering God's Presence—Jesus the Revelator

Several years ago, when I was just learning how to come into the Holy of Holies, I envisioned our five-year-old granddaughter, Annie, coming in the back door of our house looking for me. She was yelling, "Nan! Nan!" (We live in an old rambling house.) In Annie's desire to be with me, she didn't stop to see how the floors were covered or what kind of light fixture hung from the ceiling. She wasn't interested in the curtains or the furniture. Annie was looking for *me*. So she kept running through the house until she came to our bedroom and found me in my closet in the back corner of the house! Annie wanted her Nan, and she didn't get distracted from her search. She searched until she saw me and heard my voice! It didn't matter what was around her. She wanted me! Moses was like this. He was not content with angels; he wanted God's presence!

Moses said, "If Your Presence does not go with us, do not bring us up from here. For how then will it be known that Your people and I have found grace in Your sight, except You go with us?" (Exodus 33:15). Our cry is the same today.

Like Moses we are no longer content with the things God does for us—we want *Him*. We are making the journey into the presence of God. Father wants His children with Him; he has made the provision for us to draw near to Him and to dwell in His presence. Jesus is the way to the Father. John 14:6 has been a key verse in our journey: Jesus said, "I am the way, the truth, and the life. No one comes to the Father except through Me." We have access to God by the blood of Jesus! Man was created to be in God's presence and in this chapter we arrive at the Holy of Holies, the third and final division of the tabernacle. In the next three chapters we will visit the last two articles of furniture: the ark of the covenant and the mercy seat. In the last chapter we will look at the dwelling place of God and how it is God's desire for us as His children to dwell in His secret place. But in this chapter we are doing an overview of the last division of the Tabernacle, the Holy of Holies.

Let's practice what we have been studying. We will not only draw near, but let's enter into God's presence. Let's talk to Father. Conversation is the vehicle of fellowship, someone once said. Often in my quiet time in the morning I pray a prayer similar to the one below. It covers the process that the pattern of the Tabernacle teaches us. I find myself right where I long to be, in the presence of God. Find a quiet place and pray this prayer out loud to the Father with me. Let's enter God's presence together.

> *Father, we come. We come to You by the way You have provided. We know we can come running to the mercy seat. We enter Your courts today with thanksgiving in our hearts that You have made provision for us to draw near to Your presence and dwell with You. You have made provision to deal with the sin that has separated us from You.*
>
> *Father, thank You for Jesus. Jesus, You are the gate by which we enter the courts of our God—You are the door. Jesus, You gave yourself on the brazen altar. Thank You for your blood. You are the spotless Lamb whose blood has redeemed us and brought us out of darkness into this marvelous light and given us the forgiveness of sin. Jesus, it is your blood that justifies us, just as though we had never sinned and cleanses us from all sin as we walk in the light as You, Jesus, are in the light, and we have fellowship with one another.*
>
> *Thank You, Jesus, Word of God, You are our mirror, and You are the water that washes us. Your Word shows us where we need to clean up, and Your Word cleanses us! Hallelujah! What a Savior! You have terminated sin! You are the terminator!*
>
> *Thank you, Jesus. The blood and the water, the two cleansing agents, have cleansed me from sin. The*

blood and the water bear witness to the Holy Spirit. Draw us, Holy Spirit. Come, Holy Spirit. Help us find our way. Illuminate us, Holy Spirit. You are welcome here. You bring us into the holy place and illuminate the table of God and show us the fellowship we have in You, with Jesus, the Word of God on the table. Holy Spirit, You are the illuminator!

You bring to life the Word of God. You take the black ink on white paper and make it live in me. Jesus, Word of God, You are my life. It changes me and conforms me to Your image as I apply and do Your Word.

Your Word fills me and gives me fellowship with Your priests as we minister to each other and as we draw near the Golden Altar to join You, Jesus, our Great High Priest. We join You to intercede and worship. We have drawn near. You have brought us near. We don't have to worship from afar. We come boldly into Your presence. There is no veil to keep us away. We worship you, almighty God. There is none like You! We fall down and worship You. You are our God. You alone are God. You are holy. We regard You as holy. You are high and lifted up. We lift our eyes to You—we have dove's eyes, no peripheral vision. Our eyes are focused on You alone. "The things of this world grow strangely dim in the light of Your glory and grace."

Jesus, You have brought us to Father. Glory to your name! Blessed is the Lord God of Israel. Amen.

We have followed the pattern of the tabernacle, and it has brought us into the Holy of Holies, the secret place of God's tabernacle.[160]

This is the destination of our journey. This is the place where God said, "Make an ark...you shall put the mercy seat on top of the ark...and there I will meet with you and I will speak with you from above the mercy seat..."[161] In 2 Kings 19:15, we read, "Then Hezekiah prayed before the LORD, and said: 'O LORD God of Israel, the *One who dwells between the cherubim,* You are God, You alone, of all the kingdoms of the earth. You have made heaven and earth'"[162] (emphasis added).

The tabernacle of Moses shows us three distinct stages of the Christian life. The Holy Spirit will lead all those who are willing into the Holy of Holies to dwell there. The Holy Spirit has charge of the way into the Holy of Holies. It is a spiritual mystery, and He is the revealer of mysteries (1 Corinthians 2). Treasures do not lie on the top of the ground but are hidden and must be searched for to be discovered. We have come to the secret place. Secrets are not shouted from the house top, but whispered to those who have gained access to the bearer of the secret. Let's remain diligent and press into this last division of the tabernacle. A hunger for righteousness and a longing for very close fellowship with Jesus are required! The youngest believer who is hungry and thirsty can come boldly into the Holy of Holies. In Revelation 22:1 we see the pure river of water of life, clear as crystal, proceeding from the throne of God and the Lamb. The mercy seat is God's throne; the river of God flows from beneath this throne. In verse 17 we read, "And the Spirit and the bride say 'Come!' And let Him who hears say 'Come!' And let Him who thirsts come. Whoever desires let Him take of the water of life freely." We have come to the throne of God where the water of life flows freely. Let all who are thirsty come, whether the youngest believer or the oldest saint.

Description of the Holy of Holies

The Holy of Holies is the third area of the tabernacle and houses two articles of furniture occupying one and the same place: the ark of the covenant and over the ark, the mercy seat with the cherubim over it, one on each end. The holy place and the Holy of Holies are inside of the covered tabernacle proper. The area gets smaller and smaller the closer you get to God. Once you get here, to the Holy of Holies, you are in a perfect cube, ten cubits long, ten cubits wide, and ten cubits high.[163] The Holy of Holies is completely covered in gold, typifying that it is only God.

There is a difference between the holy place and the Holy of Holies. God dwells in the Holy of Holies. In the holy place the priests ministered under the power of the Holy Spirit. They ministered with each other and fellowshipped in the Holy Spirit. *But God did not dwell in the holy place.* The veil symbolized the separation of a holy God and sinful man. They cannot dwell together. Aren't we glad that Jesus tore the veil away and that now we can come boldly right into God's presence!

There is no light in the Holy of Holies other than the Shekinah glory of God, the light of God's presence. There is nothing to attract you but God Himself and nothing to distract you from Him. God planned it this way. Most of us come to God for *things*. We want blessings, we want power, we want healing; we have needs. Our needs do lead us to God, but God wants us to come to Him not just for what He gives us, but because of who He is. We seek His face, not only His hand. We want *Him*.

Enter with Boldness

The way into the Holy of Holies—into the presence of God—has been opened! O Holy Spirit, reveal to us the way of access. Come in power and bring us in! The blood of Jesus gives us access into the Holiest by opening the Holy of Holies (Hebrews 10:19–21) and sprinkles our conscience to enter (verse twenty–two).

Let us enter boldly! Let's step inside.

There is a boldness required to enter the Holy of Holies. The Christian life is lived by faith. We can't see into the Holy of Holies with our natural eyes. We must believe by faith what the Word of God has shown us. And we must be *bold*. As I have said, when I was teaching the Pentateuch in Community Bible study and was challenged to find the mercy seat, I began to find references to Hebrews 10:19—*'Therefore, brethren, having boldness to enter the Holiest by the blood of Jesus'* (emphasis added). I saw the invitation to come and I began to come even though I was ignorant of the process. But *boldness* is required. Come on, have *boldness,* don't stop. You may not understand it all, but you do see it in the Word, don't you? Let's press in right here. Ask the Holy Spirit for help. Hebrews 6:1 says, 'leaving the elementary principles of Christ let us go on or press on to maturity.'[164] It is the will of God and He gives it as a command—"Let us draw near with a true heart in full assurance of faith, having our hearts sprinkled from an evil conscience and our bodies washed with pure water (that's the blood and water from the outer court). Let us hold fast the confession of our hope without wavering, for He who promised is faithful." (Hebrews 10:22) (emphasis added). Again, we are not on a wild goose chase; those who seek God with a whole heart, find Him—every time! It is time to press in. "Not that I have already attained, or am already perfected; but I press on, that I may lay hold of that for which Christ Jesus has also laid hold of me. Brethren, I do not count myself to have apprehended; but one thing I do, forgetting those things which are behind and reaching forward to those things which are ahead, I press toward the goal for the prize of the upward call of God in Christ Jesus. Therefore let us, as many as are mature, have this mind." (Philippians 3: 12–15a). At this juncture, we have one thing on our minds: we want to be with God in His presence, in the Holy of Holies. "One thing I have desired of the Lord, that will I seek: That I may dwell in the house of the Lord all the days of my life …" (Psalm 27:4).

The Dwelling Place

We come by the "new and living way," which does not do away with the tabernacle of the old covenant but fulfills it. We come

- "By the blood of Jesus"—Hebrews 10:19 (the brazen altar)

- "With a true heart"—Hebrews 10:22 (clean at the brazen laver)

- With "full assurance of faith"—Hebrews 10:22 (the Holy Spirit illuminates the Word; we eat the Word of God and faith comes)

- "Having our hearts sprinkled"—Hebrews 10:22 (the table of showbread removes all condemnation and heaven's sweet fragrance (frankincense) covers.

We too become new—new creations with the authority of God to enter His presence! Hallelujah! We are believer priests, unashamed and unafraid, coming into God's chambers. We are coming past the torn veil, past the veil that was torn by God from top to bottom when Jesus died on the cross.[165] We are coming to worship and love our God, the God of our fathers—Abraham, Isaac, and Jacob—the God and Father of our Lord Jesus Christ. Hallelujah!

Jesus has made the way to Father. He is:

- The Way
- The Truth
- The Life

He has brought us into the presence of God, His Father! We are invited to enter boldly. We can come with even more boldness than Moses could. We have the blood of Jesus, not the blood of bulls and goats. We are invited by Jesus to abide—to dwell! The new and living way fulfills the pattern Moses gave us.

The Holy of Holies is the secret place of the most high God in Psalm 91. And the Holy of Holies is the place of abiding that Jesus talks about in John 15 and the "rest" of God the writer of the Hebrews talks about in Hebrews 4.

Just look at the benefits of dwelling in the secret place in Psalm 91. When we dwell in the secret place of the Most High we abide under the shadow of Almighty God: the almighty, all–powerful, unconquerable God, indicating God's greatness and strength and everlasting nature. He even tells us what to say: I will say of the Lord, "He is my refuge and my fortress; My God, in Him I will trust" (verse 2). Say that out loud so you can hear it until you believe what you are saying. You *will* find rest. It goes on to say that as we dwell in him, He delivers us from the things that ensnare us. He covers us; we find refuge under His wings. (Can't you just feel the warmth of that place under His wings? Down from under the wings of birds is used to fill comforters that we sleep under. I like to say that this was the first down comforter, this place under His wings. And when I go to bed at night with troubles on my mind, I crawl up under the wings of the Almighty here in this secret place and spend the night—did you know that abide means to spend the night?) Just go back and read Psalm 91 and list the benefits of dwelling here in the secret place. Health, protection—because He has set His love upon me—deliverance, He will exalt you, He will be with you in trouble and honor you and give you long life and satisfy you and show you His salvation. This is the secret place with all its benefits. That was the goal of our journey, to find the secret place. Now do you know how to get here? Just follow the pattern. It leads here every time. Show others how to come; that will make Father's heart very glad!

This is the place of abiding that Jesus told us about in John 15: "Abide in me and I in you," and He followed it with many benefits. When I abide, my prayers are answered; I bear much fruit, and that glorifies the Father. The Holy Spirit pours His love in my heart, and I am able to abide in His love and love others and keep His commandments to love Him and love my neighbors. When I find Jesus, I find everything; He is healing, peace, prosperity, and anything else I can come up with. He is my abiding place; He is my secret place. We have come into that place, the Holy of Holies, where He sits on the throne.

Well, what can we say? Christ has opened the Holy of Holies. The pattern of the tabernacle shows us "the way into the Holiest." We have followed the pattern and "here we are in Your presence, lifting holy hands to You"!

For the last few years, the Holy Spirit has been encouraging us as believers/priests to draw near to God. The Holy Spirit has given songs to present–day psalmists that lead us into the very presence of God. Coming by God's pattern gives meaning to our worship. The songs we sing take on new meaning.

> O the glory of Your presence
> We your temple give You reverence
> So arise to Your rest, and be blessed by
> our praise
> As Your presence now fills this place
> As we glory in Your embrace[166]

Come into the Holy of Holies
Enter by the blood of the Lamb
Come into His presence with singing
Worship at the throne of God
Lifting holy hands
To the King of kings
Worship—worship Jesus.[167]

"For a day in Your courts is better than a thousand" (Psalm 84:10). We have found what our souls long for—here in Your presence. We don't have to ask, "Are we there yet?" We know we are in His presence.

God has restored the priesthood. Judson Cornwall said, "As a result of the new birth, we become priests by lineage, son–priests, as were Aaron's sons; through faith we become believer–priests, somewhat akin to the Levites, but by personal and intimate relationship to God, rather than through lineage or office, very much like Moses. Toward the end of Christ's earthly relationship with the eleven faithful disciples he told them: 'Ye are my friends … henceforth I call you not servants; for the servant knoweth not what his lord doeth: but I have called you friends' (John 15:14–15, KJV). So the New Testament saint has access to the Holy of Holies by lineage, by faith, and by an intimate relationship."[168]

As a result of the new birth, we are "born priests" just like the sons of Aaron and just like with Moses and Abraham. Jesus wants to be friends with us in a personal, intimate relationship. We are friend/priests—priests with our High Priest, Jesus. We are invited to "come boldly"—a fearless, faith-filled approach to replace the fear-driven Old Testament approach.

We don't want to become content with knowledge—we want to know Christ, the crucified Christ *and* the risen Christ! God has called us to grow up, to mature. We must come to the cross, and we must never lose sight of the power Jesus released by being obedient, even to death on the cross. But Jesus is not on the cross any more; He's on the throne. We must move past just wanting knowledge, always learning, delighted with sermons and books but never getting beyond the stage of being fed. We need to get up from the table (the golden table of showbread) and use what we have received to help others and to come on into the presence of God and minister to the Lord. Let's grow up and move from always needing help to being a help for others as God's kingdom of priests! Hunger for righteousness and a longing for a very close fellowship with Jesus is required!

Are we there yet?

When we come into the Holy of Holies we come into the place where God is. Just like Annie pursuing and staying with it until she got in to the place where her grandmother was, it is Him that I have been seeking all along. He is the Lord of glory. He is the one I have been seeking and drawing near. And here I am—where He is. The secret place is where He dwells. I bow down in worship and say, "You are my God." The experience is based on the reality that Jesus is the Ark of God. He is the Mercy Seat. He is in me, I am in him, and we are in the Father. We are making the transition in to the Holy of Holies. We have two more pieces of furniture to visit. They are all God. This is the best part of all. There is no light here but the light of his Presence and the light that shines from the lampstand since the veil was removed.

Father, we come boldly into Your presence! How awesome and wonderful You are!

CHAPTER 10

The Ark of the Covenant— Jesus, My Ark

The Holy Spirit has led us right into the presence of the most high God, God Almighty, to be in the place of His dwelling. The articles of furniture in the tabernacle are just like the works of Jesus in that they are signs designed to point us to Him—to His dwelling place, the Holy of Holies! As Pastor Eddie Turner said, "The signs show us how to get the real thing." Jesus has brought us to the Father, and we know how to follow the signs to come back into His presence forever! The New Testament saint is invited into the Holy of Holies where Jesus, our Great High Priest, bids us to enter boldly with His blood! He has made full provision and has given us a personal invitation![169] We have access to the King of glory.

We have come past five articles of furniture, each representing the works that Jesus accomplished to provide our great salvation. We have stopped at the brazen altar, the brazen laver, the golden lampstand, the golden table of showbread, and the golden altar of incense. If we have been doers of the Word and have applied what we have learned, we have been cleansed of sin by the blood of Jesus and the washing of God's Word; we have been filled with the power of the Holy Spirit and the Bread of Life, and the Holy Spirit is helping us to worship and pray.

We have come past the outer court and the holy place, and we can—we are able—to enter the Holy of Holies by the blood of Jesus! Hallelujah! Because of His blood, we have access to God. I can access God; I have access into the mighty presence of God. We are able to come in where no one in Israel could, except the high priest once a year. Jesus has given us access to God and the Holy Spirit has shown us the way! We have come into the Holy of Holies and will be visiting the last two articles of furniture: the ark of the covenant covered by the mercy seat—the two are never separated. (The mercy seat will be the last article we visit. We will consider it in the next chapter.)

Description of the Ark of the Covenant

The ark was a rectangular chest three feet nine inches long and two feet three inches wide and high. It was made of acacia wood overlaid with gold inside and out and had a gold rim around the top.

Ark of the Covenant, covered by the Mercy Seat

The ark of the covenant housed three items: the two tablets of stone (the Law), the golden pot of manna, and Aaron's rod that budded.[170] The ark covered by the mercy seat was the first article of furniture that Moses was instructed to build and is symbolic of God's throne and his presence. The tabernacle was built for the ark so that God could dwell among his people.[171] God's glory dwelt in the Holy of Holies.[172]

The Two Tablets of Stone
God's law is represented by the two tablets of stone that were in the ark. It was on these stones that God wrote the Ten Commandments. God gave these tablets of stone to Israel but by the time Moses came down from the mountain with them, Israel was already breaking the first commandment by idolatry. In anger, Moses cast down the tablets and they were broken. God,

in his mercy, called Moses to come up the mountain again. The next time Moses went up to the mountain, the Lord, the God of the second chance said, "Cut two tablets of stone like the first ones, and I will write on these tablets the words that were on the first tablets which you broke" (Exodus 34:1). This time Moses was not allowed to display the tablets to Israel but was commanded to put them inside the ark (Exodus 25:16, Deuteronomy 10:2). They were then covered by the mercy seat. God knew man was incapable of keeping the law, so He covered the law with his mercy (Exodus 40:15).

God's law is as unchanging as God Himself. His law is eternal. The two tablets of stone—God's law—are the expression of God's own righteousness. Psalm 40:7–8 tells us about this law in its relation to Christ and is quoted in the epistle to the Hebrews; this refers to Jesus. "Then I said, 'Behold I come; in the scroll of the book it is written of me. I delight to do Your will, O my God, and Your law is written within my heart.'" The ark containing the two tablets of stone represents Christ with God's law in His heart. Jesus never deviated by a hair's breadth from the eternal law of God's righteousness.

Man could not keep the law by his own efforts. He tried once and failed before the law even got down the mountain, and God covered the law in the ark with the mercy seat! We will see the mercy seat in the next chapter. The ark covered by the mercy seat foreshadowed what Jesus would accomplish on the cross for all who would believe. It is not by you keeping the law; it's Christ in you keeping the law. You can't do it in your own strength any more than the children of Israel could! The law in His heart is the only way of righteousness. Romans 3:20 states, "Therefore by the deeds of the law no flesh will be justified in his sight, for by the law is the knowledge of sin." Don't fall back to standing and looking at the two tablets of stone and saying, "Okay, God, I'll do it." The devil will prove you a liar before the words are out of your mouth. Keeping the law is a way of righteousness that has been excluded once for all. Never take the lid off the ark and go back to trying to keep those tablets of stone. God's way is in the ark in you, and the law in the ark, Christ being the ark.[173] The great mystery is revealed, Christ in you, the hope of glory.

- Jesus fulfilled the law to the letter—Matthew 5:17

- He bore the curse of the law—Galatians 3:13

- He is the end of the law for everyone who believes—Romans 10:4

Now Hebrews 8:8–11 unfolds this truth of Christ having the law in His heart. In verses eight and nine,

God sets aside the first covenant to introduce the second.

> Because finding fault with them, He says: "'Behold, the days are coming,' says the LORD, 'when I will make a new covenant with the house of Israel and with the house of Judah—not according to the covenant that I made with their fathers in the day when I took them by the hand to lead them out of the land of Egypt; because they did not continue in My covenant, and I disregarded them,' says the LORD."

That covenant was set aside because Israel broke it before it was even finalized.

Verse ten continues with, "For this is the covenant that I will make with the house of Israel after those days, says the LORD: I will put My laws in their mind and write them on their hearts; and I will be their God, and they shall be My people." There is the condition for being God's people—not that you have God's law on two tablets of stone hanging on the wall, but that they are written on your heart. That's what makes you a member of God's people. When we receive Jesus, the ark of God finds home in our hearts. That Ark, Jesus, houses the law of God. Therefore when Jesus is in my heart, the law of God is in me! Verse eleven states, "None of them shall teach his neighbor, and none his brother, saying, 'Know the LORD,' for all shall know Me, from the least of them to the greatest of them."

Paul, speaking about his ministry, says in 1 Corinthians 9:20–21:

> And to the Jews I became as a Jew, that I might win Jews; to those who are under the law, as under the law, that I might win those who are under the law; to those who are without law, as without law (not being without law toward God, but under law toward Christ), that I might win those who are without law.

What Paul is actually saying is that we are in the law *in Christ*. Christ is the keeper of the law for us. When Christ rules our hearts, then God's law rules our hearts *through Christ in our hearts*. We really are totally dependent on Christ! Christ in us, the hope of glory![174] O rule, King of glory—come in and rule in my heart!

The Golden Pot of Manna

The second item housed within the ark was the golden pot of manna. During the time that the children of Israel were in the desert, God provided them with food—manna.[175] We learned at the golden table of showbread that Jesus is the manna. In John 6:48–51, Jesus said,

> "I am the bread of life. Your fathers ate the manna in the wilderness, and are dead. This is the bread which comes down from heaven, that one may eat of it and not die. I am the living bread which

came down from heaven. If anyone eats of this bread, he will live forever; and the bread that I shall give is My flesh, which I shall give for the life of the world.

Jesus is very clearly saying, "I am the true manna, the true bread that came down from heaven." Then in verse fifty–seven of that same chapter, he makes a tremendous statement: "As the living Father sent Me, and I live because of the Father, so he who feeds on Me will live because of Me." In essence, Jesus is saying that we have life by our union with the Father. He says, "The one that believes in Me will have life by union with Me, as I have union with the Father. In that union with Me, he shall feed upon Me and I will be the hidden manna in his heart; on that manna he will feed day by day." Jesus is the revelation of the Father. Jesus reveals Father to us! To me! "At that day you will know that I am in My Father, and you in Me, and I in you" (John 14:20).

In Revelation 2:17a, Jesus speaks to believers in the church, and He gives them the promise of hidden manna: "He who has an ear, let him hear what the Spirit says to the churches. To him who overcomes I will give some of the hidden manna to eat." That's the manna in the gold pot! Supernatural revelation! We feed on Christ, the manna, by our inner spiritual communion with him. Feeding on Him, we live by Him as He lives by His union with the Father. This is the inward spiritual union with Christ whereby He becomes the hidden manna in our heart. Bread of heaven, feed me 'til I want no more! O, Jesus, you satisfy me!

Aaron's Rod That Budded

The third item in the ark is Aaron's rod that budded. We can read about this rod in Numbers 17:1–11. Aaron's authority as high priest was challenged by the leaders of the tribes in Israel. God settled the challenge once and for all. God instructed Moses to tell the leader of each tribe to write his name on his own rod and bring it to the ark. God validated Aaron's authority as high priest by causing his rod to sprout buds, blossoms, and almonds. The rod is a symbol of authority, and Aaron's rod is a type of God's authority, attestation, and revelation. The name on that rod today is not Aaron, but Jesus. By the resurrection God vindicated the claim of Jesus. He brought forth blossoms, buds and almonds, so to speak, in that one experience. The rod is divine *attestation,* and it comes by divine revelation.

> Word study: *attestation;* from attest, Webster's defines it as: to bear witness to; to certify, declare to be correct, true, or genuine.[176]

When you have revelation and attestation you have authority. When you say, "thus says the Lord," that's authority. It isn't about shouting; it's having been in revelation and coming out with attestation.

Meaning of the Three Items

The three items inside the ark—the tablets of stone, the manna, and the rod are a type of worship, fellowship, and revelation.

- Worship—it is by worship that we come into the presence of God. Worship is not necessarily sounds we utter but more an attitude of the heart. Every single word in Hebrew or Greek that is translated "worship" indicates a position of the body: the bowing of the head, the bowing of the body from the waist, and the prostrating of the whole body, that demonstrates the inward, the unseen, position of the heart. So worship is not primarily praise; it is the attitude with which you approach God. Worship relates to those tablets of stone. Worship is the total submission to the righteous law of God. That law, just like the stone it was written on, doesn't change, doesn't bend, and doesn't deviate. It is through complete reverence that we approach God. As Leviticus 10:3 says, "He is holy," He is righteous, He is God. I bow, bend to His holiness, His righteousness, His Godhead. Consider the Lord's Prayer. It doesn't begin with petitions; it begins with attitude: "Hallowed be your name. Your kingdom come. Your will be done."[177] This attitude shows that we are bowing lower and lower before almighty God.

This relates to John 14:15. Jesus said, "If you love Me, keep My commandments." In John 15:7 Jesus states, "If you abide in Me, and My words abide in you, you will ask what you desire, and it shall be done for you." His will, His kingdom, and his name. Most of us go straight to the petitions without the access. The first half of the Lord's Prayer is all about access; *then* come the petitions. This is worship: a worshipper doing God's will. That is the one that God will hear! The approach to God is being in submission to the eternal unchanging law of God, which is Christ's being in our hearts. We are yielding to the King. Yes! The King rules a kingdom—the kingdom of God. He is the King of glory. This is what the tablets of stone symbolize: the righteousness of God. We bow before His righteousness; we humble ourselves and yield to His way.

- Fellowship—comes out of and after our approach to God in worship. Without worship we don't have fellowship. God won't fellowship with someone who approaches irreverently or hastily. God is a God of total righteousness. When we approach with worship, we enter into fellowship and begin to feed upon the manna in the golden pot. This is fellowship—this is the hidden manna. Jesus, the ark, brings me into fellowship with God almighty.

He calls to me, "Open the door. Let Me come in and fellowship" (Revelation 3:20).

- Revelation—out of worship and fellowship come revelation. We receive revelation of the mind, will, and purpose of God. The rod that budded symbolizes the supernatural power of God bearing witness to, certifying, and declaring in us the attestation of God. The rod that budded is the "stamp of approval" God has placed upon us. [178] The shekinah glory of God illuminates this place! Wow! O, the glory of Your presence.

Jesus, the Ark

The ark typifies the person of the Lord Jesus Christ. It was made of acacia wood found throughout the tabernacle. Acacia is incorruptible wood, typifying the humanity of Jesus. It was overlaid with gold, typifying the deity of Jesus—the perfect combination of true humanity and true divinity is the union of the two natures. Only Jesus is qualified to bring God and man together. His blood is God's blood. That's how the blood of Jesus has redemptive power! Jesus is God!

All of the other articles of furniture outside this room speak of his work. The ark speaks of Christ as a person, as did other arks in Bible history: the one that preserved Noah and his family and the one that preserved Moses as a baby. Those arks spoke of Christ symbolically but more for what He did than for Christ as a person. The ark of the covenant speaks of Christ as a sweet, intimate friend.[179]

The following, concerning Jesus as the ark, is taken from Derek Prince's tape series entitled *The Way into the Holiest:* "The Ark is Christ revealed to the spirit, or Christ within your own spirit, since your spirit, in this way of interpreting it, is the Holy of Holies. There is a place in you where Christ is to dwell in the Spirit. The Ark in the Bible is always a type of Christ."

Derek Prince further illustrates this by comparing two arks—the great ark of Noah and the little ark of Moses—in this way:

- The Great Ark
  - Typifies you in Christ. For salvation, you enter into Christ by faith. God closes the door and in Christ you pass through the waters of baptism, which is an essential part of total salvation. The waters of baptism represent our separation from the ungodly world, just as Noah's ark was protected from the waters of the great flood. Just as Noah, we step out into a new world, new covenant, new sacrifices, and new laws. The ark of Noah is a vivid picture of water baptism: entering into Christ the Ark and in Christ passing through the waters and coming forth to begin a new life. Romans 6:4 tells us, "Therefore we were buried with

Him through baptism into death, that just as Christ was raised from the dead by the glory of the Father, even so we also should walk in newness of life."

- The Little Ark
  - Typifies Christ in you, the hope of glory.[180] It is this: "I have been crucified with Christ; it is no longer I who live, but Christ lives in me; and the life which I now live in the flesh I live by faith in the Son of God, who loved me and gave Himself for me" (Galatians 2:20).

Both arks illustrate New Testament relationships, but the ark of the covenant reveals the person of Jesus Christ far more than His purpose or what He has done for us."

Jesus Christ is my ark, my sweet, intimate friend. "In that day you shall know that I am in the father and He in me and I in you." (John 14:20) He is in me. I am in Him. We are in the Father! He is my hiding place, my strong tower, my refuge from the storm. He is my secret place, *the* secret place. He puts the law of God in my heart. He is the hidden manna that I feed on. He is God's revelation to me and reveals God to me. I wish I could describe Him! In the Holy of Holies we are in the secret place of the most high God, in the presence of God almighty.

Knowing You, Jesus, knowing You
There is no greater thing.
You're my all; you're the best
You're my joy, my righteousness
And I love You, Lord.[181]

We need to accept His invitation and come to Him—all the way—not just drawing near as in Hebrews 4:16, but entering boldly into the Holiest, finishing our journey as in Hebrews 10:19. Jesus is in me, and I am in Jesus and we are in the Father![182] Then our perspective can be real. When we know Him, His works are even sweeter! Where He is, His works are. He is the treasure we seek. Jesus is my exceeding great reward.[183]

Let's make it a priority to make the person of Jesus our focal point and not just the work He accomplished.

Our needs have drawn us to God, but at the same time our needs have kept us from drawing near—what a paradox! We have become satisfied in having our needs met, and the enemy deceives us with our own satisfaction. Because our needs have been met, we often stop pressing toward and pursuing God. We fail to enter. Sometimes we are lazy; apathy sets in—we grow weary. The cares of this world consume us, and we lose focus.

Sometimes it is the "traditions of men" that keep us from pursuing God. Sometimes our leaders fail to encourage us in our pursuit because they themselves have not experienced true intimacy with God.

The good news is that we have been ruined! We have tasted the best now, so we can't settle for less than Your presence, Lord! "Oh, taste and see that the LORD is good" (Psalm 34:8). Nothing else but God himself can satisfy us because we have tasted of Him already! We must see Him—open our eyes, Lord; we want to see Jesus! We want Him; He is our desire! I believe the Holy Spirit is shifting our focus from the work of Jesus to the person of Jesus.

The ark, Jesus Christ, is the foundation for the mercy seat. Our destination is God's mercy seat. The throne of God, the mercy seat, rests upon the ark. God covers the Law, His righteousness; and the rod, His authority; and the manna, true revelation, with Himself—with His great mercy. The mercy seat, our next chapter, is our destination, but the mercy seat and the ark are joined forever. God's mercy covers the ark of God! Hallelujah!

We are the generation longing to see Your face, Father God, Your glory. King of glory, Lord of hosts, Lord mighty in battle, we seek Your face! You are our God! The Holy Spirit is inspiring songs of worship that are the songs of our hearts, like "Draw Me Close to You," "Open the Eyes of My Heart," and many others. We long to draw near to You, Lord Jesus!

The Holy of Holies is all about God. It is His dwelling place—square, the same in every direction, representing His unchanging nature. It is all gold, representing His deity. The Holy of Holies was located in the center of the tabernacle which was located in the center of the camp: The LORD thy God in the midst of thee is mighty, he will sing and rejoice over thee with joy, he will rest in His love, he will joy over thee with singing, the Lord thy God in the midst of thee is mighty, is mighty, is mighty! (Zephaniah 3:17).

Entering Rest

Jesus is our ark—He is our center. He is in the midst of us! He is in the midst of me! (Just say that out loud: "Jesus, ark of God, You are in the midst of me. The Lord my God in the midst of me is mighty, is mighty, is mighty!") We are in Him, and He is in us.[184] This is the throne room, the King's chambers. The Lord of glory is on the throne, and we fall down and worship Him. We lay all that we are before Him. We worship Him. This is where you belong, child of God. "Here my heart is satisfied—within Your presence. I sing beneath the shadow of Your wings." We are made for God's presence; His presence is the place of rest. Don't fall short—enter His rest.[185] Don't just be a hearer of the Word, be a doer of the Word. Enter in beyond the veil—not in heaven, but now. Today is the day of salvation.[186]

We New Testament Christians are very much like Aaron and his sons and spend far too much time in the outer court, serving the needs of the people and never going beyond the basic plan of salvation Jesus provided for by His work on the cross and through the Word. Many times we so desire to have our needs met that we fail to see the Person who meets them. We see only the provision, and we stop short of the Provider. We miss the real treasure—God Himself, who resides in the Holy of Holies over the ark. But God is opening the eyes of our heart, and our desire is to see Him, the King of kings and Lord of lords, not just to enjoy His benefits. Let's go past benefits and enter into His rest…"since a promise remains of entering his rest, let us fear lest any of you seem to have come short of it…be diligent to enter that rest" (Hebrews 4:1, 11a).

Let's get past provision. We can have relationship with the King. Now we can come boldly, having our consciences sprinkled by the blood of Jesus. Therefore, let us enter!

Our last stop will be at the mercy seat that covers the ark. There we will encounter the loving God alone—none but He is our hope. See you at the mercy seat—the throne of God.

Let's pray.

O Father, thank You for Jesus, my ark! Holy Spirit, you have brought us into the Holy of Holies—I draw near; I come running! Father, as we draw near, I know that You are drawing near to us![187] *It is more than I can comprehend—You want me with You! I know that I need You, but Your love for me is amazing.*

Thank You for revealing Your great love to me through Jesus Christ, my Lord, by the power of the Holy Spirit. Pour the love of God in my heart—my desire is to love You with all my heart, soul, mind, and strength.

Jesus, thank You for giving Yourself for me.

Thank You for Your blood that has brought me out of darkness into this marvelous light. Thank You that it is Your blood that has justified me and put on me the robe of righteousness just as though I had never sinned. Wow!

Thank You that as I walk in the light as You are in the light the blood of Jesus cleanses me from all sin and gives me fellowship with the body of Christ.

Thank You for the Word of God that is a mirror; I can see what I need to let Your Word wash off of me.

Thank You for the Holy Spirit, who shines and illuminates the Word of God and makes it alive to me. Your Word feeds my soul and causes me to be conformed to You.

Thank You, Holy Spirit, for helping me pray and worship. Thank You for revealing Jesus to me and for showing me the way to Father, the way into the Holiest. Here my heart is satisfied! My God, I love You! Amen.

CHAPTER 11

The Mercy Seat—the Secret Place
of the Most High God

Welcome to the mercy seat—the place of appointment. God said, "You shall put the mercy seat on top of the ark … and there I will meet with you." [188]

God is the God of mercy. It is to the mercy seat, the throne of grace, that God has called us to draw near. God did not choose to dwell at the brazen altar in the outer court, nor did He make His presence known from the ark; it is at the mercy seat that God chose to dwell. Our journey has brought us to the mercy seat. We have reached our destination. We come boldly to the throne of grace to

- Receive mercy
- Find grace

Jack Hayford has said in his commentary in the New Spirit–Filled Life Bible at Hebrew 4:16, "Come boldly literally means 'without reservation, with frankness, with full and open speech.' We approach a throne of grace, not of judgment, obtaining mercy for the past and grace for the present and future."[189]

> Word Study: *mercy*, in *Webster's Unabridged Dictionary* is defined as: kindness in excess of what may be expected or demanded by fairness; a disposition to forgive; forbearance and compassion.

> Mercy is "compassionate to those in trouble, even if their trouble is their own foolish making."[190]

We serve a *merciful* God. It's the mercy of God almighty that is so amazing! It is here at the mercy seat I find mercy so real, that I know that my relationship with God is because of His relationship with me; it is because He has shown me such great mercy. Mercy takes care of the offense, and it pardons the transgression. Compassion feels the need; mercy fills the need! Come, receive mercy; find grace. This is God's plan! His plan all along was to get us to the mercy seat!

The Mercy Seat—God's Throne

The mercy seat was made of solid gold—wholly and absolutely God. Gold is a type of divine glory. (Types are not used to establish doctrine but to illustrate doctrine already established by the Scriptures.) The mercy seat was formed of beaten gold, very much like the lampstand. Exodus 37:6–9 gives us the description:

He also made the mercy seat of pure gold; two and a half cubits was its length and a cubit and a half was its width. He made them of one piece at the two ends of the mercy seat: one cherub at one end on this side, and the other cherub at the other end on that side. He made the cherubim at the two ends of one piece with the mercy seat. The cherubim spread out their wings above, and covered the mercy seat with their wings. They faced one another; the faces of the cherubim were toward the mercy seat.

Everything on the mercy seat was formed from one solid piece of gold, even the two cherubs who faced each other and bowed to face God. It was beaten into shape from one lump of solid gold much like the golden lampstand—one solid piece including the cherubim. (The lampstand and the mercy seat are the only two pieces of furniture in the tabernacle that are solid gold.) Its dimensions were exactly the same as the ark's: three feet nine inches long and two feet three inches wide. The mercy seat fits the ark perfectly and covers it. The ark and the mercy seat are made for each other. The ark holds the law of God and is covered by mercy. Psalm 85:10: mercy and truth have met together; righteousness and peace have kissed! Peace and reconciliation through Christ, the mercy seat. The mercy seat is a type of Christ in His highest revelation—it shows Him in His relationship to God the Father. This is

Jesus and the Father—God–Man (wood overlaid with gold) and God (pure gold).

The Mercy Seat covering the Ark of the Covenant

The mercy seat has the exact same measurements—width and length—as the top of the ark and fits exactly inside the gold crown that is around the ark. This crown proclaims Jesus Christ—Son of Man, Son of God, King of kings, Lord of lords—Jesus Christ our mercy seat—the place of rest for the restless, sin–laden soul. "Come to Me, all you who labor and are heavy laden, and I will give you rest," Jesus said in Matthew 11:28. The deity and humanity of our King are inseparable! The mercy seat is the only chair in the tabernacle. This is the place of God's rest.

The two cherubim made of hammered gold are at the two ends of the mercy seat, one piece with the mercy seat. Their wings are stretched out above, covering the mercy seat. They face one another and the mercy seat. The cherubim guard and administer; they are agents of God's mercy. Genesis 3:24: "He [God] placed the cherubim at the east of the garden of Eden … to guard the way to the tree of life," and as we find in Ezekiel 10, they are closely related to the glory of God. Ezekiel 10:4: "The glory of the Lord went up from the cherub, and paused over the threshold of the temple; and the house was filled with the cloud and the court was full of the brightness of the Lord's glory."

The merciful God has made Himself accessible. What a privileged people we are as God's children! We have access to God! The tabernacle of Moses is the pattern of God's plan to restore fellowship between God and man. God revealed his plan in Exodus 25:17–22:

> "You shall make a mercy seat of pure gold; two and a half cubits shall be its length and a cubit and a half its width. And you shall make two cherubim of gold; of hammered work you shall make them at the two ends of the mercy seat. Make one cherub at one end, and the other cherub at the other end; you shall make the cherubim at the two ends of it of one piece with the mercy seat. And the cherubim shall stretch out their wings above, covering the mercy seat with their wings, and they shall face one another; the faces of the cherubim shall be toward the mercy seat. You shall put the mercy seat on top of the ark, and in the ark you shall put the testimony that

I will give you. And there I will meet with you, and I will speak with you from above the mercy seat, from between the two cherubim which are on the ark of the testimony, about everything which I will give you in commandment to the children of Israel."

All other pieces of furniture in the tabernacle point to the mercy seat. All other ministries prepare the believer to come to the mercy seat.

El Roi—the God Who Sees

It was here on the mercy seat that God dwelt among the children of Israel.[191] The ark, covered by the mercy seat was God's beginning place. God sees the end from the beginning. God sees![192] He knew we would "miss it,"[193] and He made a way for us to return.

The mercy seat is where God started. Man can contribute nothing to his salvation. God does it all— wholly. From the beginning, Jesus said, "No one can come to Me unless the Father who sent Me draws him" (John 6:44). John Bevere has a chapter called "God's Pursuit" in his book *Drawing Near*.[194] In it he says: "He [God] actually yearns for us. (See James 4:5). The word yearn means to long for intensely. This has been His deepest heart cry since the beginning of time ... A people who would desire to know Him in response to His desire for us! David relates the awesome reflection God has for each of us in Psalm 139:17–18: "How precious are your thoughts about me, O God! They are innumerable! I can't even count them; they outnumber the grains of sand!" (NLT). It is almost impossible to grasp, but His thoughts about each one of us are more than all the grains of sand on the earth! Think on it a moment.

Salvation is God's idea, and He provides the full package. God is full of mercy. God reveals to man the salvation He has provided for him step by step. We have heard the call; we have accepted the invitation God has given us to draw near, to enter into the Holy of Holies. Andrew Murray said, "It is a call to all luke-warm, half–hearted Christians, no longer to remain in the outer court of the tabernacle content with the hope that their sins are pardoned, nor even to be satisfied with having entered the holy place, and there doing the service of the tabernacle, while the veil still hinders the full fellowship with the living God and his love. It calls to enter in through the rent veil, into the place into which the blood has been brought and where the High Priest lives, there to live and walk and work always in the presence of the Father. It is a call to all doubting, thirsting believers who long for a better life than they have yet known, to cast aside their doubts and to believe that this is what Christ has indeed done and brought within the reach of each one of us: He has opened the way into the holiest! This is the salvation that He has accomplished, and which He lives to apply in each of us, so that we shall indeed dwell in the full light of God's countenance."[195]

O my! To dwell in the full light of God's countenance!

God Almighty—to Abide under the Shadow of the Almighty

We have come into the King's chambers, to the mercy seat, to the throne of God, the secret place of the most high God to abide under the shadow of the Almighty. O, yes! It is *way* too good to be true! But it *is* true— God wants His children with him, and it is His plan and His provision that has given us access into His presence. The ark and the mercy seat are joined—once joined, never to be separated. Here my heart is satisfied within Your presence. I sing beneath the shadow of Your wings. Hallelujah! Enter into the joy of Your Lord!

We have followed the pattern:

- We have received forgiveness of sin—the brazen altar

- We have washed in the water of the Word—the brazen laver

- We are filled with God's Spirit—the golden lampstand

- We have partaken of the bread of his face in fellowship—the golden table of showbread

- We worship Jesus, our great High Priest, and join Him in intercession—the golden altar of incense

- We come with Jesus into the presence of Father to abide in the ark under the mercy seat of God—the ark of the covenant covered by the mercy seat

Jesus has brought us to the Father. Jesus is the way to the Father. Do you feel the *rest?* Remember in Exodus 33:14, God said, "My Presence will go with you, and I will give you rest."

Jesus, the Mercy Seat

Jesus is the mercy seat—He is one with the Father. In John 10:30, Jesus said, "I and My Father are One"; His purpose is Father's purpose. "Behold, I have come … to do Your will O God" (Hebrews 10:7). Jesus delights to do Father's will. Jesus suffered as God and became our mercy seat! Only the mercy seat and the lampstand are made of solid gold, but the mercy seat is preeminent. God did not choose to dwell in the holy place; He dwells on the mercy seat between the cherubim. Jesus is our shield from the heat of judgment; He accepts what we deserve. He is our propitiation—the word *propitiation* describes Christ, through His sacrificial death, as appeasing (pacifying) the wrath of God on account of sin.

Romans 3:24–25 tells us: "Being justified freely by His grace through the redemption that is in Christ Jesus, whom God set forth as a propitiation by His blood, through faith, to demonstrate His righteousness, because in His forbearance God had passed over the sins that were previously committed." The Greek word translated here as *propitiation* is the same word translated as *mercy seat* in Hebrews 9:5!

> Word Study: *mercy seat, hilasterion* (hil–as–*tay*–ree–on); Strong's #2435:[196] Although used only here (Hebrews 9:5) and in Romans 3:25 in the N.T., the word is quite common in the Septuagint, where it primarily denotes the mercy seat, the lid of gold above the ark of the covenant. In this verse it has that meaning, indicating the place of atonement. The root meaning of *hilasterion* is that of appeasing and placating an offended god. Applied to the sacrifice of Christ in that regard, the word suggests that Christ's death was pro-pitiatory, averting the wrath of God from the sinner.[197] (The Septuagint version is a Greek translation of the Old Testament.)

- First John 2:2 uses the same word—and He Himself is the propitiation (mercy seat) for our sins, and not for ours only but also for the whole world.

And also the same word in

- First John 4:10. In this is love, not that we loved God, but that He loved us and sent His Son to be the propitiation for our sins.

God declares that Christ Jesus is the propitiatory, the mercy seat, a constant declaration that sins of the past have been paid in full. How good is that? We are completely justified through the blood of Jesus—just as though we had never sinned.[198] We are new creatures in Christ![199] Our sin is paid in full by our wonderful bridegroom King; in other words, God's judgment against sin has been put aside through the atoning sacrifice of Christ and now He can show mercy to believers. The judgment seat becomes the mercy seat because of the power of Jesus's blood to justify sin. We saw Jesus become our propitiation at the cross, the brazen altar, as God's bleeding Lamb—accepting God's wrath for our sin and meeting the demands of the law. We have seen Jesus at the brazen altar as the perfect Lamb, at the brazen laver as the Word of God, at the lampstand as the light of the world, at the table of showbread as the table that holds the bread and as the bread of his face, at the golden altar as our Great High Priest, and here in the Holy of Holies as the ark of God and the mercy seat. God chose not to abide on the brazen altar in judgment. Rather, He chose to dwell on the mercy seat—He made himself available to us in His mercy.

- He promised to dwell in the Holy of Holies

- This seat is His dwelling place

- He inhabits the space between the faces of the cherubim

- He is enthroned on mercy

Here, at the mercy seat, where God is at rest, it is Jesus Christ who is our shield. His work pleased Father so much that Father accepted it *for us*. Hallelujah—we can come running to the mercy seat of God! Because of the work of Jesus on the cross, His blood is brought here to the mercy seat, blotting out even the remembrance of our sin. His blood alone was able to satisfy the judgment of God against us. Now we can abide in Christ—dwell in the secret place of God almighty!

God's Throne—the Throne of Grace

God's seat—this throne—is sprinkled with Jesus' blood, and our holy God dwells among an unholy people. Jesus, because of what He accomplished with His blood, declares us to be righteous,[200] and we are a royal priesthood, a holy nation.[201]

God accepted the blood of Jesus that was sprinkled on this seat

- on His throne
- in His heaven
- by His High Priest

Christ died to place God's throne among us. God sits on the throne—He is Lord—He is the ruler of all the earth and He is the judge of all the earth. The mercy seat is the judgment seat, and the kingdom of God proclaims Jesus is King in His birth and in His death (Matthew 2:2; 27:37). The atoning blood, the sprinkled blood, transforms a throne of judgment to the throne of grace. The mercy seat was in the center of the tribes of Israel. God in the midst of his people: "The Lord thy God in the midst of thee is mighty" (Zephaniah 3:17, KJV). The tribes of Israel were arranged in the formation of the cross, with God in the center. God had a plan all along, and He is able to bring His plans to pass.

This throne, the mercy seat, is God's resting place. Hebrews 1:3 tells us that Jesus "sat down at the right hand of the Majesty on high." And Hebrews 10:12–14 says of Jesus, "But this Man, after He had offered one sacrifice for sins forever, sat down at the right hand of God, from that time waiting till His enemies are made His footstool. For by one offering He has perfected forever those who are being sanctified." He dwells here in the Holy of Holies and is available to us here at His dwelling place between the faces of the cherubim. He lives in us, and we live in Him. Listen to what Jesus said in John 14:20–21: "At that day you will know that I am in My Father, and you in Me, and I in you. He who has My commandments and keeps them, it is he who loves Me. And he who loves Me will be loved by My Father, and I will love him and manifest Myself to him."

If it were not for the blood of Jesus, God could not be in our midst. But the mercy seat, His throne, is sprinkled with the blood of Jesus. The high priest was instructed in Leviticus 16:14: "He shall take some of the blood of the bull and sprinkle it with his finger on the mercy seat on the east side; and before the mercy seat he shall sprinkle some of the blood with his finger seven times." Jesus, our Great High Priest, has sprinkled His own blood for us; that blood is speaking for you today, right now.[202] When our sin is under the blood, we find mercy. No blood, no mercy.

We can enter boldly into the presence of God; the price has been paid. We have access to the throne of God—to God himself, his presence! O hallelujah! Hallelujah to the spotless Lamb of God! My Jesus, you are mine!

Judson Cornwall has said, "Our evil hearts of unbelief, our seared consciences, our prideful hearts, and the vain imaginations of our minds all need repeated applications of the blood ... at the mercy seat we are enabled to make fresh appropriation of the blood when standing in His holy presence. In spite of all the cleansings of the outer court our inner lives need faith's appropriation of the purging blood. This is done as we stand worshipfully in God's presence at the blood–soaked mercy seat."

We might say as we journey into the presence of God:

- At the brazen altar we meet Jesus
- At the golden lampstand we meet Holy Spirit
- At the mercy seat we commune with Father

In the holy place we commune with the Holy Spirit and are able to commune with the priests and minister at the altar of incense with Jesus our High Priest, but here at the mercy seat we commune with Father God. Remember, God's ultimate purpose has always been to have communication with man. God has longed for fellowship with man, and He has made the way—He provided it for himself and for us. Jesus made the way. Jesus said in John 17:21, "that they all may be one, as You, Father, are in Me and I in You; that they also may be one in Us, that the world may believe that You sent Me."

God's plan does not only deal with man's sin but provides restoration of fellowship between man and his God. The putting away of sin is necessary to access fellowship with God and unity with the Father and the Son. As we draw near, God produces the necessary changes; as this happens, we become capable of responding to Him, and we enjoy His presence. God's purpose is realized at the mercy seat—the meeting place. God is waiting for you to come! Revelation 21:3 states, "Behold, the tabernacle of God is with men, and He will dwell with them, and they shall be His people. God Himself will be with them and be their God." Let everyone who is thirsty come! In Revelation 21:6–7 Jesus says, "It is done! I am the Alpha and the Omega, the Beginning and the End. I will give of the fountain of the water of life freely to him who thirsts.

He who overcomes shall inherit all things, and I will be his God and he shall be My son."

Unity—Fellowship and the Glory
Christ's atoning work that covered the broken law was covered by the two cherubim, one at each end. Their faces point inward, toward the mercy seat, and their wings bow forward to touch exactly over the center of the mercy seat, the place where God reveals His glory. Again, the three activities are represented here as they were in the ark are:

- Worship—the bowed wings of the cherubim are a type of worship, the bowed position of the body

- Fellowship—their faces toward one another are fellowship—face to face

- Revelation—where the wings meet, and the faces meet, God reveals His glory

Worship and fellowship—there God reveals Himself. There God places His glory. Just as Jesus said in Matthew 18:15–20, first we forgive and get right with our brother. That brings unity—we are facing each other—wingtips touching.[203] Then in verses nineteen through twenty he says, "Again I say unto you that if two of you agree on earth concerning [the King James Version says, "as touching"] anything that they ask, it will be done for them by My Father in heaven. For where two or three are gathered together in My name,

I am there in the midst of them." That is fellowship in God.

- Our faces toward one another
- And toward the mercy seat
- Touching each other, touching God—fellowship

We face one another; and in unbroken fellowship we touch, and we get what we ask for! "There, over the mercy seat I will meet with you."[204] This is where God's glory was manifested. Do you think this secret place could be what Jesus had in mind when He said, "When you have shut your door, pray to your Father who is in the secret place; and your Father who sees in secret will reward you openly" (Matthew 6:6)?

Jesus wants us to experience His glory. John 17:24 says: "Father, I desire that they also whom You gave Me may be with Me where I am, that they may behold My glory which You have given Me; for You loved Me before the foundation of the world."

God had revealed His glory to Moses in Exodus 34:5–7 when He caused all of His goodness to pass before him. Bob Mumford said it like this in his book, *The Agape Road:*

> When Moses asked God to *show him His glory,* God said He would proclaim the *name* of the Lord before him (Exodus 33:18–19). God then, in self–revelation, explains to Moses the content

of His glory which is His seven hidden attributes: "And the Lord descended in the cloud and stood there with him as he called upon the name of the Lord. Then the Lord passed by in front of him and proclaimed, 'The Lord, the Lord God *compassionate,* and *gracious, slow to anger* and *abounding in lovingkindness* [mercy] and *truth;* who keeps *lovingkindness* [faithful] for thousands, who *forgives* iniquity, transgression and sin'" (Exodus 34:5–7).

God's DNA

- Compassion

- Grace

- Slow to anger

- Mercy

- Truth

- Faithful

- Forgiving—iniquity, transgression, sin

God's character or DNA is the content of His glory and the significance of His Name.[205]

It was here at the mercy seat that God came and His presence dwelt. After the tabernacle had been set up and arranged and Moses had followed the pattern—then the glory came (Exodus 40). And in Exodus 40:34 we read, "Then the cloud covered the tabernacle of meeting, and the glory of the LORD filled the tabernacle."[206] He said in Leviticus 16:2, "I will appear in the cloud above the mercy seat." This speaks of the shekinah[207] glory, or the glory of the Lord—a flame of glory surrounded by a cloud—that came to rest on the mercy seat between the cherubim. The light in the Holy of Holies came from God himself. We have come out of the natural light of the outer court, into the illumination of the Holy Spirit in the holy place, and into the light of God himself in the Holy of Holies.

Jesus revealed God's glory, being full of grace and truth. John 1:14 states, "And the Word became flesh and dwelt among us, and we beheld His glory, the glory as of the only begotten of the Father, full of grace and truth."

When we come into God's presence, we are changed—just as it says in 2 Corinthians 3:18: "But we all with unveiled face, beholding as in a mirror the glory of the Lord, are being transformed into the same image from glory to glory, just as by the Spirit of the Lord." God is challenging us in this generation to "Arise, shine; for your light has come! And the glory of the LORD is risen upon you. For behold, the darkness shall cover the earth, and deep darkness the people; but the LORD will arise over you, and his glory will be seen upon you" (Isaiah 60:1–2). Our voices join with the prophet Habakkuk, and we declare, "The earth will be filled with the knowledge of the glory of the LORD, as the waters cover the sea" (Habakkuk 2:14). Let your purpose and plan be fulfilled! O, God!

We have come into the Holy of Holies, the place where God revealed Himself between the two cherubim—the place where the cloud descended and the glory of the Lord filled the tabernacle. God says, "I am the end. I am here. There is nothing to seek here but Me." That's why many people never come in—they want something *besides* God. In here, it's God alone. When I find Him, I find healing, peace, prosperity...He is my all.

My Story

When I read in Exodus 25:21–22, "You shall put the mercy seat on top of the ark...and there I will meet with you, and I will speak with you from above the mercy seat, from between the two cherubim" and I saw that it is at the mercy seat that God meets and speaks, I found the reference to Hebrews 10:19, "Therefore, brethren, having boldness to enter the Holiest by the blood of Jesus." I began to come by faith, saying to Father, "I see Your Word. I don't know how, but I enter boldly." It was when I "saw" this verse that I began my search to find the mercy seat and to find how to get into the presence of God. As I began to seek God, I found the pattern that has revealed the way into God's dwelling place. God is approachable! It was this verse that presented the challenge to me to find the place where God meets and speaks. Where is the mercy seat? How do I get there? I must find the answer! The pursuit of those answers led me to the pattern of the tabernacle. Now I know I always have access to God's presence, and I can show you the pattern too. And you can show those you love.

He is always available! I come running with my conscience sprinkled. I want you, Father. I have not been disappointed. I have found what my soul has longed for in you Jesus, in your presence, oh Lord!

Are we there yet?

Well, we have made it to our destination. We no longer have to ask, "Are we there yet?" For here my heart is satisfied in Your presence. I have found what my soul has longed for. I am satisfied with you, my God. Now we have access to the life we need to live here on earth, the life that satisfies our soul—His presence. He pours our hearts full of love by the Holy Spirit.[208] It is here that God enables us to do the first commandment: love the Lord our God with all our heart, soul, mind, and strength. We are incapable of doing it on our own strength, but God has provided the way for us. He will fill our hearts, and we can give back to Him the love He has given us; we are able to love others because He gives the love!

As I prepared this study, I thought of John 14:3: "If I go and prepare a place for you I will come again and receive you to Myself; that where I am there you may be also." I wondered, could that be now as well as in heaven? Now I know that Jesus has prepared a place for me on earth!

Andrew Murray said,

O the glory of the message. For fifteen centuries Israel had a sanctuary with a Holiest of All into which, under pain of death, *no one might enter.* Its one witness was: man cannot dwell in God's presence, cannot abide in his fellowship. And now, how changed is all! As then the warning sounded: *Enter Not!* So now the call goes forth: *Enter In!* The veil is rent; the holiest is open; God waits to welcome you to His bosom. Henceforth you are to live with Him. This is the message of the Epistle: Child! Thy Father longs for thee to enter, to dwell and to go out no more forever.

Oh, the blessedness of a life in the holiest! Here the Father's face is seen and His love tasted. Here His holiness is revealed and the soul made partaker of it. Here the sacrifice of love and worship and adoration, the incense of prayer and supplication is offered in power. Here the outpouring of the Spirit is known as an ever–streaming, overflowing river, from under the throne of God and the Lamb. Here the soul, in God's presence, grows into more complete oneness with Christ, and more entire conformity to His likeness. Here, in union with Christ, in His unceasing intercession, we are emboldened to take our place as intercessors, who can have power with

God and prevail. Here the soul mounts up as on eagle's wings, the strength is renewed and the blessing and the power and the love are imparted with which God's priests can go out to bless a dying world.[209]

O Father, I run into Your bosom—the shelter under Your wings. Jesus has brought us to the mercy seat. Jesus is the gate into the heart of the Father. He has opened the door into Father's heart, into the treasure chamber of God. Jesus has sweetly and gladly opened Father's heart, and there He unfolds to us the hidden riches.

> *How wonderful!*
> *How marvelous!*
> *And my song shall ever be*
> *How wonderful!*
> *How marvelous!*
> *Is my Savior's love for me!*[210]

I love the house where You live, O Lord; the place where Your glory dwells! We will conclude our study in the next chapter with a final look at the dwelling place.

CHAPTER 12

Seeking to Dwell—Abiding in God's Presence

We began our journey by asking, where is the secret place and how do I get there? The pattern of the tabernacle of Moses has given us the answer to both questions. But the end of the journey is only the beginning of learning to dwell in the King's chambers, in the presence of the King.

We no longer have to ask, "Are we there yet?" We know where we are and how we got here. My heart is satisfied within Your presence, oh Lord. Thank You for leading me into the secret place.

Let's enter the gates with thanksgiving.

O God, thank You for Your great love. It cost You more to open the Holy of Holies than I know. You have made access to God our privilege and responsibility. Lord, I long to dwell, not just to visit.

I sing to You, Lord…

> *Who am I that you are mindful of me?*
> *That You hear me when I call*
> *Is it true that You are thinking of me?*
> *How you love me—it's amazing.*
> *God Almighty, Lord of Glory*
> *You have called me friend.*[211]

We have finished our journey into the tabernacle of Moses—the pattern into the presence of God. It is no longer a mystery but a way to be followed. Now we need to come into God's presence and bring others.

Father, may I dwell in the secret place? I hear a resounding, "Yes, you may; I have prepared this place for you. I receive you to Myself that where I am there you may be also."

Father, may I "dwell in the house of the Lord all the days of my life"? O, yes, this is Father's desire. His will is in His Word. Let's take a look at what the Word of God has to say about the children of God dwelling in His presence.

Seeking to Dwell—the Place of Abiding

The psalmist who wrote Psalm 91 was most likely Moses; he knew about God's presence and the provision found in abiding under the refuge of His wings in the secret place. Psalm 91 says, "He who dwells in the secret place of the Most High shall abide under the shadow of the Almighty." We are no longer seeking to find the secret place, but we are seeking to *dwell in* the secret place! God wants us to dwell, to abide in His presence, not to just come for an occasional visit.

In Psalm 27:4–5, David states his desire to dwell in God's presence.

> One thing I have desired of the LORD,
> That will I seek:
> *That I may dwell* in the house of the LORD
> All the days of my life,
> To behold the beauty of the LORD,
> And to inquire in His temple.
> For in the time of trouble
> He shall hide me in His pavilion;
> In the secret place of His tabernacle
> He shall hide me;
> He shall set me high upon a rock.
> (emphasis added)

Psalm 24:3–5 tells us simply who may ascend into the hill of the Lord and who may stand in His holy place to dwell in God's presence.

> Who may ascend into the hill of the LORD?
> Or who may stand in His holy place?
> He who has clean hands and a pure heart,
> Who has not lifted up his soul to an idol,
> Nor sworn deceitfully.
> He shall receive blessing from the LORD,
> And righteousness from the God of his salvation.
> This is Jacob, the generation of those who

seek Him,
Who seek Your face.
Lift up your heads, O you gates!
And be lifted up, you everlasting doors!
And the King of glory shall come in.
Who is this King of glory?
The LORD strong and mighty,
The LORD mighty in battle.
Lift up your heads, O you gates!
Be lifted up, you everlasting doors!
And the King of glory shall come in.
Who is this King of glory?
The LORD of hosts,
He is the King of glory.

This Psalm gives us four things that are required to ascend the hill of the Lord and to stand in his holy place:

- Clean hands—washed with the Word
- A pure heart—cleansed by the blood
- No idols
- No deceit

This is the generation that seeks God's face. We are that generation. Throw open the gates of your heart and lift up the doors, and the King of glory shall come in!

The psalmist tells us who may abide in the Lord's tabernacle and dwell in His holy hill in Psalm 15.

Lord, who may abide in Your tabernacle?
Who may dwell in Your Holy hill?
He who walks uprightly,
And works righteousness,
And speaks the truth in his heart;
He who does not back bite with his tongue,
Nor does evil to his neighbor,
Nor does he take up a reproach against his friend;
In whose eyes a vile person is despised,
But he honors those who fear the Lord;
He who swears to his own hurt and does not change;
He who does not put out his money at usury,
Nor does he take a bribe against the innocent.
He who does these things shall never be moved.

The Throne Room

We have entered the Holy of Holies, the throne room of God, the place of abiding. The throne room is what the Apostle John saw in Revelation 4:1–3.

> After these things I looked, and behold, a door standing open in heaven. And the first voice which I heard was like a trumpet speaking with me, saying, "Come up here, and I will show you things which must take place after this." Immediately I was in the Spirit; and behold, a throne set in heaven, and One sat on the throne. And He who sat there was like a jasper and a sardius stone in appearance; and there was a rainbow around the throne, in appearance like an emerald.

God's habitat, His throne, is where He is always found. The throne was the first thing John saw. It was the authority of God that he first encountered, and it is God's authority that we must embrace if He is to dwell with us. Authority is the right to rule, govern, and control our lives. God wants us to seek first His kingdom and His righteousness.

"Make ready your heart! Make ready your home! Make ready the people of God!"[212] Prepare the way!

In Revelation 4–5, John reveals four things that God requires in his habitat.

1. Give Him the throne
   —Revelation 4:2

2. Acknowledge His holiness
   —Revelation 4:8

3. Give Him an "attitude of gratitude"
   —Revelation 4:9

4. Give Him the "Amen"—agree with God
   —Revelation 5:14[213]

- Give Him the throne. If God is going to reside in your house or in mine, if we are going to experience the fullness of His presence the way we desire, then He demands the throne. It's just that simple—the throne is God's dwelling place. He demands the right to govern, the right to control our lives. When God comes to reside, He comes as Lord, Master, and King! He must truly reside on the throne of our lives. We must be without hesitation or equivocation if His presence is to be fully manifested in us. We have changed kingdoms; King Jesus has delivered us from the domain of darkness and translated us into the kingdom of His love.

- Acknowledge His holiness. As John's eyes adjusted to his surroundings, he saw the throne of God surrounded by holiness. "Holy, holy, holy, Lord God Almighty, Who was and is and is to come!"[214] God is thrice holy, and He demands holiness from us.[215]

- Give him an "attitude of gratitude." God dwells in the midst of continual thanksgiving. It is a significant part of His habitation. (See Revelation 4:9, 1 Chronicles 16:34, Ephesians 5:20, and 1 Thessalonians 5:18.) What does God smell in your sanctuary? The aroma of thankfulness.

  o Giving thanks was a regular part of Jewish worship in the tabernacle, the temple, and the homes of the faithful. The early Christians learned to live and breathe thankfulness. What about you? Is the voice of constant thanks heard in the temple of your heart? If God sniffed the air of your sanctuary, would He smell the sweet, fragrant incense of praise and thanksgiving or the stench of bitterness, anger, pride, and ingratitude? (See Psalm 22:3.) Praise and thanksgiving are part of the habitation of God. When we gather together in a spirit of genuine praise, thanksgiving, and worship from pure and sincere hearts, we create an atmosphere that actually draws the presence of God and also individually when we offer up to God a heart and life that are pure, holy, thankful, and completely surrendered to his lordship.

- Give Him the "Amen." (See Revelation 5:12–14.) Amen means "so be it." Radical obedience. This is agreement with God—no complaining backtalk.

Conclusion

We have learned the way to abide in Christ, to dwell in His presence. We are to not just visit, but inhabit. No longer depending on others to get us there, not waiting for special meetings, we come into the presence of God because we have learned the way. And we are not the first ones to learn these principles—many have gone before us and have pointed us in the right direction. Now we can do the same! We are aware of the requirements. Have we made the decision to abide? Make your heart God's home—forever His habitation! You may dwell in His house all the days of your life.

We have come through the cross, to the throne that Jesus might work in us the power of the heavenly life, imparting that life to us. I get to know Him here in his chambers in the power of His resurrection and the fellowship of His suffering. I see Him with Isaiah, Ezekiel, Daniel, John, and the Shulamite maiden as my bridegroom king, not just my Risen Savior. Isaiah 6:1–3 says,

> "I saw the Lord sitting on a throne, high and lifted up, and the train of his robe filled the temple … above it stood seraphim … and one cried to another and said: 'Holy, holy, holy, is the Lord of hosts; The whole earth is full of His glory!'"

Song of Songs 5:16: "Yes, he is altogether lovely. This is my beloved, and this is my friend!" O my goodness! I agree with Andrew Murray: "The the worship and fellowship of a heavenly Christ makes heavenly Christians."[216] I come near and the Holy Spirit pours love in my heart for me to go out and dispense to others. I see the beauty of the bridegroom king and become willing to sell all I have to be with Him where He is. The cleansing and the filling provided by the journey prepare me to be with Him, to know Him, and to rule with Him! He has plans for me here on earth.

So here I am, Jesus. Teach me your ways from Your throne, the King's chambers. You are the bridegroom king who has brought me into Your chambers! I can breathe in the sweet fragrance of Your love. I want to know You. "Your love is better than wine. Because of the fragrance of your good ointments, your name is ointment poured forth ... Draw me away! We will run after you. The King has brought me into His chambers" (Song of Songs 1:2–4).

This is the Holy of Holies and the King of kings has a song of all songs to sing to His beloved bride. Come near and let Him draw you into His chambers. Let Him sing His song to His bride here in the Holy of Holies!

Who is like You, O Lord, among the gods?
Who is like You, glorious in holiness
Fearful in praises, doing wonders?
You stretched out Your right hand;
You in Your mercy have led forth
the people whom you have redeemed;
You have guided them in Your strength
to Your holy habitation. ...
You will bring them in and plant them
In the mountain of Your inheritance,
In the place, O Lord, which You have made
For Your own dwelling,
The sanctuary, O Lord, which
Your hands have established.
The Lord shall reign forever and ever.

Exodus 15:11, 13, 17–18

Amen.

Suggested Reading

Cornwall, Judson, *Let Us Draw Near*. Bridge Publishing, Inc., South Plainfield, NJ, 1977.

Murray, Andrew, *The Holiest of All*. Fleming H. Revell, Grand Rapids, MI, 1993.

Mumford, Bob, *Agape Road*. Destiny Image Publishers, Shippensburg. PA, 2002, 2006.

Prince, Derek tape series The Way into the Holiest.

Prince, Derek. *Atonement*. Chosen Books, Grand Rapids, Michigan, 2000.

Endnotes

Chapter 1

1   Daniel 2:22, 28

2   See also Matthew 13:11

3   New International Version Bible

4   Hebrews 9:1–14

5   Taken from Strong's Exhaustive Concordance of the Bible

6   1 Peter 2:9

7   Leviticus 10:3

8   Taken from Strong's Exhaustive Concordance of the Bible

9   Psalm 24:8, 10

10   Amos 3:7

11   1 Corinthians 2:7, 9–10

12   2 Corinthians 1:22; Ephesians 1:14

13   Hebrews 9:1

14   Hebrews 8:5; 9:23–24

15   Exodus 20:18–19

16   Exodus 20:20

17   Matthew 27:51

18   Chris Tomlin, "Better is One Day," Passion, Better is
      One Day, Sparrow Records, 1999

19   Tim Hughes, "Here I Am to Worship," Here I Am
      to Worship, Worship Together, 2001

Chapter 2

20   Exodus 25:9 comment in The Spirit Filled Life
      Bible, NKJV–1991

21   Taken from The New Spirit–Filled Life Bible, Word
      Wealth at Numbers 10:12

22   Strong's Exhaustive Concordance of the Bible

23   Hebrews 6:1, Philippians 3:12

24   Jeanne Wilkerson, *Contact with God*, Tulsa, OK,
      Harrison House, 2001 by Brent Olsson, page 52

25   Exodus 26:33, 27:9

26   Exodus 27:9–19

27   Hebrews 9:2, Exodus 26:33

28   Exodus 26:33

29   Exodus 27: 9–18

30   Ephesians 2:4–7

31   Exodus 40:3, 5, 8

32   Hebrews 10:19

33   Hebrews 9:22b

34   1 Peter 2:9

35 Ephesians 5:26

36 Exodus 25:22

37 Hebrews 4:16

38 Exodus 40:34, 36

39 Hebrews 10:19

40 Exodus 25:8–9

41 Hebrews 8:5

42 Exodus 27:16

43 John 10:7

44 2 Corinthians 5:21

Chapter 3

45 In different translations of the Bible, the terminology
    for words is different. Brazen altar or bronze altar, for
    example, are the same.

46 Strong's Exhaustive Concordance of the Bible

47 Revelation 22:17

48 Hebrews 9:22

49 2 Corinthians 5:21

50 Leviticus 1:2

51 Taken from The New Spirit–Filled Life Bible, Word
    Wealth at 2 Kings 12:9

52 Strong's Exhaustive Concordance of the Bible

53 Derek Prince *Atonement* pages 11–12

54 Hebrews 9:13–14

55 Hebrews 9:11

56 Isaiah 43:25

57 Matthew 27:51

58 Hebrews 9:21

59 1 John 1:7

60 Taken from the New Spirit–Filled Life Bible, Word Wealth at Romans 3:24

61 2 Peter 3:8

62 see Acts 3:19 and Hebrews 9:13,14

63 These "exchanges" are taken from Derek Prince, Atonement, Grand Rapids, MI, Chosen Books, 2000

64 Exodus chapters 25, 26, 27

65 Hebrews 10:19

66 Elisha A. Hoffman, "Are You Washed in the Blood of the Lamb?" 1878

67 Colossians 3:1–3

Chapter 4

68 Exodus 38:8

69 Revelation 1:5

70 Psalm 24:3–4

71 See John chapter 13:1–17

72 Ephesians 5:26, John 17:17

73 Revelation 5:10

74 Exodus 30:17–21

75 Exodus 40:32

76 This paragraph is paraphrased largely from Derek Prince, tape series entitled *The Way into the Holiest*

77 1 Corinthians 11:31

78 Hebrews 9:22

79 Colossians 2:11–12

80 Exodus 30:20–21

81 John 1:29

82 Philippians 3:12–14

Chapter 5

83 Andrew Murray, *The Holiest of All,* Fleming H. Revell, Grand Rapids, MI, 1993

84 Colossians 1:13

85 Exodus 26:31–33

86 Mark 15:37–38

87 Derek Prince, tape series entitled *The Way into the Holiest*

88 Andrew Murray, *The Holiest of All*

89 Strong's Exhaustive Concordance of the Bible

90 Taken from the New Spirit–Filled Life Bible, Word Wealth at Acts 7:33

91 New American Standard Bible

92 1 John 5:6

93 John 14:16–17; 15:26–27

94 Words in italics mine—from *Holiest of All,*
    by Andrew Murray

95 James 4:8

96 Andrew Murray, *Holiest of All,* page 310

97 Hebrews 4:16

Chapter 6

98 Exodus 25:31–40

99 John 16:14

100 Judson Cornwall, *Let Us Draw Near,* page 97,
    Bridge Publishing, Inc. South Plainfield, NJ, 1977

101 Ephesians 6:18

102 John 6:32–35, 47–51, 53

103 Psalm 141:2

104 Judson Cornwall, *Let Us Draw Near,* page 96

105 Strong's Exhaustive Concordance of the Bible

106 Taken from the New Spirit–Filled Life Bible,
    Word Wealth at John 14:16

107 Taken from Derek Prince, *The Spirit–Filled Believer's
    Handbook,* page 194

108 1 Corinthians 12:13

109 Matthew 28:19

110 John 1:29–34 and Matthew 3:11

111 Catherine Marshall *Beyond Ourselves* page 87

112 Romans 4:17

113 1 Corinthians 3:16

114 Romans 5:5

115 Matthew 22:37–38

116 John 16:14–18

117 Exodus 20:18–20

118 Luke 11:13

Chapter 7

119 Judson Cornwall, *Let Us Draw Near,* page 106,
     Bridge Publishing, Inc., South Plainfield, NJ, 1977

120 Leviticus 21:6

121 Leviticus 24:9

122 Strong's Exhaustive Concordance of the Bible

123 Leviticus 24:8

124 Leviticus 2:15–17, 24:6–7

125 Leviticus 24:5–9

126 John 6:51, 56–57

127 See Romans 12:2

128 Philippians 2:6–11

129 John 6:56

130 Romans 12:2

131 Hosea 4:6

132 Strong's Exhaustive Concordance of the Bible

133 Taken from The New Spirit–Filled Life Bible, Word Wealth at Acts 19:20

134 Taken, in part, from the New Testament Greek Lexicon

135 Derek Prince, *How to Enter the Holiest of All,* a tape series

136 *Acting On the Word* is taken in part from Gloria Copeland, *God's Will for You,* pages 25–26

137 Matthew 4:4

138 1 John 3:1

Chapter 8

139 Psalm 24:6

140 Mark 12: 30–31

141 Romans 8:26

142 Leviticus 4:7–8, 18

143 Exodus 30:6

144 Exodus 30:34

145 Leviticus 16:12–13

146 Psalm 141:2

147 Exodus 30:8, Hebrews 7:25 (Jesus), and Romans 8:26–27 (The Holy Spirit)

148 Exodus 30:7–8

149 Leviticus 16:13

150 Leviticus 16

151 11 Corinthians 1:30–31 and Hebrews 13:12 ("sanctify" means holy, or set apart)

152 Strong's Exhaustive Concordance of the Bible

153 Taken from the New Spirit–Filled Life Bible Word Wealth at 2 Kings 12:9

154 Hebrews 4:16

155 Exodus 30:7

156 Zephaniah 3:17

157 John 12:3 and Matthew 26:7

158 Hebrews 9:8, 10:19

159 Craig Smith, "Draw Me Closer, " Your Kingdom Come, Hosanna Music, 2000

Chapter 9

160 Psalm 27:5

161 Exodus 25:10a, 21–22. See also Psalm 80:1

162 See also Isaiah 37:16

163 Fifteen feet square

164 For clearer understanding read Hebrews 5:12 through 6:1

165 Matthew 27:51

166   Steven L. Fry, "Oh The Glory of Your Presence", Birdwing Music, 1983

167   Dave Browning, "Take Me In", Glory Alleluia Music, 1986

168   Judson Cornwall, *Let Us Draw Near,* page 141, Bridge Publishing, Inc., South Plainfield, NJ, 1977

Chapter 10

169   Hebrews 10:19

170   Hebrews 9:4

171   Exodus 25:8–10

172   Psalm 80:1, Exodus 25:22, 1 Samuel 3:3, 1 Samuel 4:4

173   Deuteronomy 10:1–5

174   Colossian 1:27

175   Exodus 16

176   Webster's Dictionary

177   Luke 11:2

178   Much of this section is credited to Derek Prince's tape series *The Way into the Holiest*

179   Taken in part from Judson Cornwall *Let Us Draw Near,* page 141

180   Colossians 1:27

181   "Knowing You, Jesus," by Graham Kendrick

182   John 14:20

183 Genesis 15:1

184 John 17:21

185 Exodus 33:14 and Hebrews 3–4

186 2 Corinthians 6:2

187 James 4:8

Chapter 11

188 Exodus 25: 21–22

189 Jack Hayford, *The New Spirit Filled Life Bible,* commentary at Hebrews 4:16, Thomas Nelson Publishers, Nashville, Tennessee, 1991

190 Devotional Word Studies, Dick Mills quoting C. Leslie Mittion—from Mercy, Harrison & Landsman

191 Refer to the following Scripture verses: 1 Samuel 4:4, 2 Samuel 6:2, 2 Kings 19:15, Psalm 80:1, Isaiah 37:16, Exodus 29:42–43; 30:6, 36, Leviticus 16:2, Numbers 17:4, Numbers 7:89

192 Genesis 16:13

193 Romans 3:23

194 John Bevere, *Drawing Near,* Thomas Nelson Publishers, Nashville, Tennessee, 2004, page 10

195 Andrew Murray *The Holiest of All* chapter LXXXI

196 Strong's Exhaustive Concordance of the Bible, used by permission

197 Taken from Word Wealth at Hebrews 9:5, New Spirit–Filled Life Bible

198 Romans 5:1–9

199 2 Corinthians 5: 17

200 2 Corinthians 5: 21

201 1 Peter 2: 9

202 Hebrews 12:24

203 Exodus 25:20–22

204 Exodus 25:20–22

205 Bob Mumford, *The Agape Road*—page 22, Destiny Image Publishers, Shippensburg. PA, 2002, 2006

206 See also Leviticus 9:6, 23

207 We learned earlier that the word *shekinah* is not found in the Bible but means the dwelling presence of God

208 Romans 5:5

209 Andrew Murray *The Holiest of All*

210 "My Savior's Love," Charles Gabriel, 1905

Chapter 12

211 "I Am a Friend of God," Israel Houghton and New Breed, "Another Level", Integrity Music, 2004

212 Prepare the Way, song written by Darrell Evans and Eric Nuzum

213 This whole section from "They Drank from the River and Died in the Wilderness" by David Ravenhill

214 Revelation 4: 8

215 Leviticus 11:45

216 Andrew Murray, *The Holiest of All*

listen|imagine|view|experience

AUDIO BOOK DOWNLOAD INCLUDED WITH THIS BOOK!

In your hands you hold a complete digital entertainment package. Besides purchasing the paper version of this book, this book includes a free download of the audio version of this book. Simply use the code listed below when visiting our website. Once downloaded to your computer, you can listen to the book through your computer's speakers, burn it to an audio CD or save the file to your portable music device (such as Apple's popular iPod) and listen on the go!

How to get your free audio book digital download:

1. Visit www.tatepublishing.com and click on the e|LIVE logo on the home page.
2. Enter the following coupon code:
   1177-595c-633f-0c88-f7c3-10f7-24d2-5fca
3. Download the audio book from your e|LIVE digital locker and begin enjoying your new digital enter-tainment package today!